I0142097

Galatians

A Theological Interpretation

A. Blake White

Books by

A. Blake White

The Law of Christ: A Theological Proposal

The Newness of the New Covenant

Galatians

A Theological Interpretation

A. Blake White

5317 Wye Creek Drive, Frederick, MD 21703-6938
phone: 301-473-8781 or 800-376-4146 fax: 240-206-0373
email: info@newcovenantmedia.com
Website: www.newcovenantmedia.com

Galatians: A Theological Interpretation

Published by:

New Covenant Media
5317 Wye Creek Drive
Frederick, Maryland 21703-6938

Orders: www.newcovenantmedia.com

Printed in the United States of America

ISBN 13: 978-1-928965-36-7

Dedication:

To Larry Newcomer,
my faithful pastor.
Thank you for your
humility and generosity.

Table of Contents

TABLE OF CONTENTS XI

ACKNOWLEDGEMENTS XIII

CHAPTER 1: INTRODUCTION TO GALATIANS 1

CHAPTER 2: GALATIANS 1:1-10 7

CHAPTER 3: GALATIANS 1:11-2:14 21

CHAPTER 4: GALATIANS 2:15-3:5 41

CHAPTER 5 GALATIANS 3:6-14 57

CHAPTER 6: GALATIANS 3:15-25 69

CHAPTER 7: GALATIANS 3:26-4:7 87

CHAPTER 8 GALATIANS 4:8-20 105

CHAPTER 9: GALATIANS 4:21-5:1 119

CHAPTER 10: GALATIANS 5:2-15 135

CHAPTER 11: GALATIANS 5:16-26 155

CHAPTER 12: GALATIANS 6:1-10 175

CHAPTER 13: GALATIANS 6:11-18 193

CONCLUSION 207

Acknowledgements

I am indebted to many teachers, as all of us are. I want to highlight one in particular: Tom Schreiner. I took a course with him on the Greek exegesis of Galatians that was a delight from start to finish. Dr. Schreiner is an excellent teacher, but he is also a *godly* teacher. Anyone who knows him speaks of his humility and kindness. Also, he is a churchman. At the time I am writing, he teaches, writes like crazy, and pastors a church. His heart in his writing is to honor God by edifying the church. I have learned much about Galatians and Pauline theology in particular from Dr. Schreiner. I encourage interested readers to buy anything he has written. Although I am sure Dr. Schreiner would not agree with much of what I have written, his fingerprints are on every page.

Thanks to Mills Road Baptist Church for being eager to learn and live this sweet letter.

I also want to thank my lovely wife, Alicia. You are a Proverbs 32 woman and I am grateful to God for you.

May God give us all grace to "obey the truth" (Gal 5:7).

Chapter 1: Introduction to Galatians

Before we embark on our journey through this magnificent letter, it's always good to take a step back to consider the wonder of what we are doing. We in America have a huge privilege. The Word of God is widely available and we are free to study and teach it. What gratitude we should have when holding our own copy of the Holy Scriptures! Seriously, this is the Word of the living God. This is the God who made caterpillars and camels, bears and bees, and the seas and all that is in them. This is the Word of the God who holds all things together, and he has spoken *to us*. Amazing! Let's dive in.

Introduction

There is not much debate concerning who wrote the letter to the Galatians. All agree it was the Apostle Paul. The audience of the letter however, is greatly debated. If one has an interest in that sort of thing, consult any standard commentary where you will probably find more information than you ever wanted. For what it's worth, I tend to think the South Galatian theory is correct, but ultimately, if you are reading the letter *you* are the audience. Paul had visited Southern Galatia on his first missionary journey (Acts 13-14), and many consider Galatians his earliest letter (probably written about AD 48-50).

Background

The first Christians in Jerusalem were Jewish. Jews viewed the law as an eternal end in itself. As the gospel spread, there was an increasing number of Gentiles coming to faith in the Jewish Messiah. It is not hard to see how tensions rose.

I always find it helpful to take a few steps back, to zoom out so that we don't focus too narrowly on the trees and lose sight of the forest. Anytime we are reading Scripture, we should remember that God has one plan: to bring all things to a head in Christ Jesus (Eph 1:8-10). So zoom out and consider the bigger picture. The triune God creates. Not because he needed to; because he wanted to. He creates humanity, but they rebel. Adam fails, and the next Adam, Noah, fails as well. Rebellious humanity wants to make a name for themselves but God had a different plan. He wants to make a name for a pagan named Abram (Gen 12:1-3, Josh 24:2). He promises this pagan land, offspring, and blessing, but he also commands him to be circumcised. God keeps his promises, and the first realization of the promise of offspring comes with the nation of Israel. Israel was called to be a kingdom of priests and a holy nation (Exod 19:5-6), but they were no different than Noah and Adam before them. They end up in exile due to their hard hearts, but God makes promises of a new covenant, a new exodus, a new heart, and a new creation. In Jesus Christ, these promises are coming to fruition, but the agitators in Galatia do not see the significance of his coming.

These agitators[1] crept in and did two primary things: They accused Paul of being **dependent** on Jerusalem and the twelve apostles for his gospel and accused him of **dis-**

[1] See Galatians 1:7, 5:10: *tarrassō*.

torting what they considered to be the true gospel.[2] They were saying that Gentiles must keep the old covenant law to be accepted by God. They were saying we are in need of divine assistance. Paul counters by showing we are in need of divine *rescue*.

Why do you think they were requiring people to be circumcised? Because Genesis 17:9-14 says God's people must be circumcised![3] That passage says,

> *And God said to Abraham, "As for you, you shall keep my covenant, you and your offspring after you throughout their generations. This is my covenant, which you shall keep, between me and you and your offspring after you: Every male among you shall be circumcised. You shall be circumcised in the flesh of your foreskins, and it shall be a sign of the covenant between me and you. He who is eight days old among you shall be circumcised. Every male throughout your generations, whether born in your house or bought with your money from any foreigner who is not of your offspring, both he who is born in your house and he who is bought with your money, shall surely be circumcised. So shall my covenant be in your flesh an everlasting covenant. Any uncircumcised male who is not circumcised in the flesh of his foreskin shall be cut off from his people; he has broken my covenant.*

The agitators would have appealed to their Bible! This is the way false teaching always works: misused and decontextualized proof texts! The key question to ask though is "Were they rightly interpreting the Bible?" As the letter to

---

[2] Thomas R. Schreiner, *Galatians.* ZEC. Grand Rapids: Zondervan, forthcoming.

[3] John Barclay, *Obeying the Truth: Paul's Ethics in Galatians* (Vancouver: Regent College Publishing, 1988), 53.

the Galatians will make clear, the answer is a resounding "No!"

As an aside, it is interesting to take note that Paul does not argue against the agitators in this letter. Paedobaptists[4] say that old covenant circumcision is replaced by baptism in the new covenant so infants should be baptized like (male) infants were circumcised. Note that Paul doesn't equate baptism and circumcision! If baptism were the replacement of circumcision, the easiest way to solve the Galatian problem would have been for Paul simply to say, "Dear friends, don't you know that baptism is the new sign of the covenant, replacing circumcision?" Instead, Paul says that receiving circumcision nullifies the grace of God.[5] To me, this is strong evidence that baptism does not replace circumcision in the new covenant.

The agitators (and some of the Galatians) had two main problems:

1. They had a view of people that was too optimistic. Apparently this problem is not limited to American evangelicals after all.
2. They were confused about what time it was in redemptive history.

By way of introduction, I also want to point out the "cross-centeredness" of the letter. Sometimes evangelical

---

[4] Those who baptize infants.

[5] Thomas R. Schreiner, "Baptism in the Epistles: An Initiation Rite for Believers," in *Believer's Baptism,* ed. Thomas R. Schreiner and Shawn D. Wright, (Nashville: B&H Academic, 2006), 90.

Christians are criticized for focusing too much on the cross. We respond that we major on the cross because the Bible majors on the cross! Whether or not one likes it, Christianity is *bloody*. The cross is central in Galatians:

1:4 *Christ gave himself for our sins*

2:20 *The Son of God loved me and gave himself for me*

3:1 *It was before your eyes that Jesus Christ was publicly portrayed as crucified*

3:13 *Christ redeemed us from the curse of the law by becoming a curse for us*

4:4-5 *God sent forth his Son to redeem those under the law*

5:1 *Christ has set us free*

5:11 *If I still preach circumcision, the offense of the cross has been removed*

6:12 *They are troubling you in order that they may not be persecuted for the cross of Christ*

6:14 *Far be it from me to boast except in the cross of our Lord Jesus Christ*

It should also be noted that the first commandment doesn't come until Galatians 4:12: Become like me. Isn't that significant? We live in a "do this and live" culture. Many evangelical Christians over-emphasize a "What Would Jesus Do" state of mind and neglect the "What *Did* Jesus Do" state of mind. What Jesus would do is *vitally* important but must be viewed in light of what Jesus did do. As with many of Paul's letters, the first half is usually theological, and the second half is more practical. So here, Paul lays out quite a bit of theology before he finally exhorts the church to do anything. This verse (Gal 4:12) is probably the main point of the book as well. Paul wants his hearers (which includes us) to be like him, realizing the sufficiency of the Messiah and the freedom his person and work brings.

The structure of Galatians is fairly simple:

1-2 Paul's Self Defense

3-4:11 Paul's Theological Defense

4:12-6:18 Paul's Application

Chapter 2: Galatians 1:1-10

Paul, an apostle—not from men nor through man, but through Jesus Christ and God the Father, who raised him from the dead—and all the brothers who are with me, To the churches of Galatia: Grace to you and peace from God our Father and the Lord Jesus Christ, who gave himself for our sins to deliver us from the present evil age, according to the will of our God and Father, to whom be the glory forever and ever. Amen. I am astonished that you are so quickly deserting him who called you in the grace of Christ and are turning to a different gospel—not that there is another one, but there are some who trouble you and want to distort the gospel of Christ. But even if we or an angel from heaven should preach to you a gospel contrary to the one we preached to you, let him be accursed. As we have said before, so now I say again: If anyone is preaching to you a gospel contrary to the one you received, let him be accursed. For am I now seeking the approval of man, or of God? Or am I trying to please man? If I were still trying to please man, I would not be a servant of Christ.

When we read any letter, it is always helpful to keep in mind that they were meant to be read (or heard) in one sitting. Remember that when we examine smaller sections. They must always be understood and interpreted in light of the whole letter. It only takes twenty minutes to read through Galatians. I encourage you to form the habit of reading through books of the Bible in one sitting occasionally. You will undoubtedly be refreshed.

Greeting (1:1-5)

1 *Paul, an apostle—not from men nor through man, but through Jesus Christ and God the Father, who raised him from the dead*

Paul cuts to the chase: "I am an apostle, one sent out to represent another. I am not dependent upon anyone for my ministry. I wasn't sent by any person but by Jesus Christ and God the Father. I wasn't sent by human commission or human authority. I was sent by the God of the resurrection." Right off the bat, we have a major theme here. We tend to think of the resurrection merely as proof of Christ's deity which it is, but there is more to it; it's an end-time reality. Resurrection means new creation. Jews viewed resurrection as an end-time event where God would raise all his people from the dead (Isa 26:19, Dan 12:1-3). For example, consider the famous new covenant passage of Ezekiel 36, where God promises to give his people a new heart and a new Spirit. The next chapter (37) consists of the vision of the valley of the dry bones. Ezekiel 37:12-14 says,

> *Therefore prophesy, and say to them, "Thus says the Lord GOD: Behold, I will open your graves and raise you from your graves, O my people. And I will bring you into the land of Israel. And you shall know that I am the LORD, when I open your graves, and raise you from your graves, O my people. And I will put my Spirit within you, and you shall live, and I will place you in your own land. Then you shall know that I am the LORD; I have spoken, and I will do it," declares the LORD.*

When resurrection happened, it meant God was fulfilling his end-time promises. What they did not expect was one man to be raised in the middle of history.[6] The coming of Christ brought the old age to an end. This is significant

---

[6] See N.T. Wright *The Resurrection of the Son of God* (Minneapolis: Fortress Press, 2003); Michael Gorman, *Cruciformity: Paul's Narrative Spirituality of the Cross* (Grand Rapids: Eerdmans, 2001), 320.

in Galatians because the agitators were not grasping the significance of the new age which had been inaugurated by the resurrection of Jesus. They wanted to implement the old covenant, which is part of the old age. They were confused over what time it was.

> 2 *and all the brothers who are with me, to the churches of Galatia:*

Also, Paul writes, I am not alone but have support (all the brothers and sisters with me). The agitators were accusing Paul of being on his own. People are with him though.

> 3 *Grace to you and peace from God our Father and the Lord Jesus Christ,*

Paul begins as usual, saying "grace and peace to you." Grace is central and it is the grace of God that issues in peace—shalom, wholeness. Peace with God through Christ, and peace with others through the Spirit. In Greek the word for *grace* (*charis*) is similar to the word for *greetings* (*chairein*). Paul is always thinking theologically so he changes a simple greeting so that it points to the nature of God. And of course, peace was the normal Jewish greeting.

Also notice that Jesus Christ is set on the same plane as God the Father. Nowhere does the New Testament say that grace and peace come from people or angels, but always from God. Jesus is the God-man.[7]

> 4 *who gave himself for our sins to deliver us from the present evil age, according to the will of our God and Father,*

---

[7] See Robert Letham, *The Holy Trinity* (Phillipsburg, NJ: P&R Publishing, 2004).

Paul emphasizes grace right from the start. Christ gave himself for our sins. Christ is sufficient. There is no need to add to him. We will also see later in the letter that we are called to Christ-like love. The laying down of his life is the means of forgiveness and the model for life.

This verse is a very important verse for the whole book. It under girds much of what Paul is talking about here, and what he talks about elsewhere. Jewish thought distinguished between this age and the age to come (Matt 12:32, Mark 10:30).[8] In Ephesians 1:21, Paul says that God had placed Jesus at his right hand, far above all rule and authority, power and dominion, and every name that can be invoked, not only in this age but also in the one to come.

What was new though is that through the resurrection of Christ, the ages now overlap. The age to come has invaded this present evil age. This is a vital theological foundation for the whole of Paul's thinking and therefore it should be for ours as well. Paul, in particular, often uses contrasts to make his point. Consider the following eschatological contrasts that he uses: law/faith, sin/righteousness, flesh/Spirit, letter/Spirit, slavery/freedom, death/resurrection, and more. The theological underpinnings of all these contrasts are the present age and the age to come which are headed up by the first Adam and the Last, respectively.[9] Adam is the head of the old creation and Christ is the head of the

---

[8] See Geerhardus Vos, *The Pauline Eschatology* (Phillipsburg, NJ: P&R Publishing, 1930), 38; Kim Riddlebarger, *The Case for Amillennialism* (Grand Rapids: Baker, 2003), 65-66.

[9] Jason Meyer (following Vos), *The End of the Law,* Nashville: B&H Academic, 2009, 55-56.

new. So one commentator says that Galatians is "about the death of one world, and the advent of another."[10] He even sandwiches the book with this reality: we have Galatians 1:4 at the beginning and 6:14-15 at the end, which says, "But far be it from me to boast except in the cross of our Lord Jesus Christ, by which the world has been crucified to me, and I to the world. For neither circumcision counts for anything, nor uncircumcision, but a new creation." The age to come has now arrived in the cross and resurrection, but the present evil age has not vanished entirely. The new creation has been inaugurated, but not consummated.

5 *to whom be the glory forever and ever. Amen.*

All this was in accordance with God's will and to his glory, and his glory alone. The Holy Spirit, through Paul, is very zealous to avoid mingling human glory with God's glory. Part of the problem with the Galatians' behavior is that they are downplaying the significance of Christ's sufficiency and God's glory. Again, they had two big problems: their view of people was too optimistic and they were confused over what time it was in redemptive history.

Application

- Christians throughout history have disagreed about apostolic authority. The Roman Catholic Church believes that the authority of the apostles is now bound up with the Pope, due to apostolic succession. I am still protesting and believe that the authority of the apostles is now bound up with their writings, the

---

[10] J.L. Martyn, "Apocalyptic Antinomies in Paul's Letter to the Galatians," *NTS* 31 (1985): 414, quoted in Meyer, *The End of the Law,* 56.

New Testament canon. The Bible is our authority. It is God's Word to us.

- Of course, that last point does not mean that we disregard Christian tradition though, does it? No, we are not alone in the act of interpretation.[11] We are surrounded by a great cloud of witnesses. Even Paul tells us that he has people with him (1:2). He wasn't alone. If someone has a new interpretation that has never been proposed, we ought to have red flags all around. Tradition takes a back seat to exegesis, but that doesn't mean we throw it out of the car.[12]
- We are the new creation people. The new age has dawned. The Spirit has been poured out. The church is the new order, the new humanity. Do we look any different than the people of the old creation? We, as the people of the future, ought to have values that are very different than those around us who do not have the Spirit. More on this below.

Explanation of the problem (6-10)

6 I am astonished that you are so quickly deserting him who called you in the grace of Christ and are turning to a different gospel

---

[11] See Robert Letham, *Through Western Eyes* (Great Britain: Mentor, 2007), 196-98; Timothy Ward, *Words of Life,* (Downers Grove: IVP Academic, 2009), 141-51 for helpful treatments of the relation of tradition and *sola Scriptura.*

[12] Full disclosure: I write this as a Baptist so I honor tradition, but do part ways with it on many occasions where I read Scripture differently.

Paul is surprised by what is taking place. It is shocking. It is foolish (Gal 3:1). Here, Paul uses the words "so quickly" (*takēōs*) to allude to the golden calf incident and idolatrous Israel.[13] Before Moses had even come down from the mountain, Israel was building its own god! Exodus 32:7-9 says, "Then the Lord said to Moses, 'Go down, because your people, whom you brought up out of Egypt, have become corrupt. They have been quick *(takūs)* to turn away from what I commanded them and have made themselves an idol cast in the shape of a calf. They have bowed down to it and sacrificed to it and have said, 'These are your gods, O Israel, who brought you up out of Egypt'." Paul is accusing the Galatians of doing the same here. They are turning from the one who called them and they are doing so "quickly." "Calling" here refers to God's effective work of calling his people to himself through the proclaimed gospel. Notice the means by which God calls: the grace of Christ.

7 not that there is another one, but there are some who trouble you and want to distort the gospel of Christ.

The Galatians were beginning to turn to another gospel, which is no gospel. Why does adding to the gospel nullify it? To turn to the law is not good news, but bad. As Martin Luther writes, "There is no middle ground between the righteousness of the law and Christian righteousness. Anyone who strays from Christian righteousness must fall into the righteousness of the law; in other words, when people

---

[13] Richard Longenecker, *Galatians. Word Biblical Commentary,* vol. 41, ed. Ralph P. Martin (Columbia: Nelson Reference & Electronic, 1990), 14.

lose Christ, they slip back into reliance on their own works."[14]

Paul even goes after the motives of the agitators here. They are seeking to pervert the gospel. Herman Ridderbos writes, "They apparently constituted a group of persons who, from the outside, and also probably under alien influence, resisted Paul's preaching. Their intent was nothing less than to overturn the gospel that had Christ as its content and to live out an opposing principle. This happens when the cross of Christ is no longer recognized in its all-sufficiency (cf. 5:2 ff.). Then the gospel is turned upside-down and robbed of its strength."[15]

> 8-9 *But even if we or an angel from heaven should preach to you a gospel contrary to the one we preached to you, let him be accursed. As we have said before, so now I say again: If anyone is preaching to you a gospel contrary to the one you received, let him be accursed.*

Paul throws down a serious warning here. If anyone should preach a different gospel than the one they preached before, let them be under God's curse! This is not merely a wish, but a solemn affirmation of what will certainly be the case.[16] Watch out Galatians! This is not a secondary matter here, but one of the primary truths of Christianity! Your eternal destiny is at stake.

---

[14] Martin Luther, *Galatians. The Crossway Classic Commentaries.* Edited by J.I. Packer and Alister McGrath. Wheaton, IL: Crossway Books, 1998, xxi.

[15] Herman Ridderbos, *The Epistle of Paul to the Churches of Galatia.* NICNT. Grand Rapids: Eerdmans, 1953, 49.

[16] Ibid., 50.

Why do you think he mentions angels? In Jewish tradition, it was held that angels delivered the law to Moses. Galatians 3:19 says that the law was put in place by angels through an intermediary. Hebrews 2:2 says the old covenant message was *"declared by angels."* Acts 7:53 says the law was received as delivered by angels (cf. Acts 7:38, Deut 33:2 LXX). Paul clearly wants to guard the purity of the gospel and keep it from being perverted by *anyone,* including himself!

What is the gospel? Oftentimes our tradition equates justification by faith with the gospel, which has some truth to it. Here, Paul mentions the gospel in Galatians 1:8, and will continue to expound the teaching of justification in the next couple of chapters. Also, in Galatians 3:8, the gospel announces that God will justify the Gentiles. However, the gospel is broader than justification by faith. Forgiveness of sins is at the heart of the gospel, but that is not the end of the story. We need to think about where Paul derived his understanding of the gospel (*euangelion*). First and foremost, the background is the Old Testament:

> Isaiah 40:9: *You who bring* ***good tidings*** *to Zion, go up on a high mountain. You who bring* ***good tidings*** *to Jerusalem, lift up your voice with a shout, lift it up, do not be agreed;*
>
> Isaiah 41:27: *I was the first to tell Zion, 'Look, here they are!' I gave to Jerusalem a messenger of* ***good tidings.***
>
> Isaiah 52:7: *How beautiful on the mountains are the feet of those who bring* ***good news,*** *who proclaim peace, who bring* ***good tidings,*** *who proclaim salvation, who say to Zion, 'Your God reigns!'*
>
> Isaiah 61:1: *The Spirit of the Sovereign Lord is on me, because the LORD has anointed me to preach* ***good news*** *to the poor.* (emphasis mine).

These are speaking of God's promises to his people of a new exodus (return from exile), a new covenant, and a new creation (cf. Isa 54:10, 65:17, 66:22). So these promises are clearly in mind when the New Testament uses the word *gospel*. But Paul also has his Greco-Roman world in mind as well when he speaks of the good news. It was often used of military victories. When an emperor conquered his enemies, it was hailed as good news. When a new ruler was enthroned or born, it was *gospel*.[17] It was good news. For example, in 9 BC there was an inscription of the birthday of the emperor Augustus which says, "The beginning of the joyful news *(euangelia)* for the world."[18] A new king—the true King—had arrived! In Mark 1:15, we read, "The time is fulfilled and the kingdom of God is at hand; repent and believe in the gospel *(euangelion)!*" The last Adam, the seed of Abraham, the true Davidic King has come, conquered Satan, sin, and death, reversing the effects of the fall of Adam, absorbing the curses of the covenant and was raised from the dead, ascended to the supreme place of authority, the right hand of the Creator God, and is the true ruler of the world.

Simon Gathercole has helpfully summarized the main elements that must be present when discussing the gospel.

---

[17] Gorman, *Cruciformity,* 353.

[18] D.A. Carson, "The Biblical Gospel," in *For Such a Time as This: Perspectives on Evangelicalism, Past, Present and Future,* ed. Steve Brady and Harold Rowdon, (London: Evangelical Alliance, 1996), 75; N.T. Wright, *Paul,* (Minneapolis: Fortress Press, 2005), 77; Shane Claiborne and Chris Haw, *Jesus for President* (Grand Rapids: Zondervan, 2008), 67.

He says, "The three core elements of the gospel [are] God's account of his saving activity (1) in Jesus the Messiah, in which, by Jesus' death and resurrection he (2) atones for sin and (3) brings new creation."[19]

10 *For am I now seeking the approval of man, or of God? Or am I trying to please man? If I were still trying to please man, I would not be a servant of Christ.*

After condemning anyone who would distort the gospel, it should be clear that Paul is not trying to please people. Typically, if you want to please people, threatening them with eternal condemnation is not the best way to go. No, no, no. Paul is a servant of Christ. His aim in all things is to please God (1 Cor 10:31). He is not a people-pleaser.

Application

- Repent and believe the gospel. Jesus is king of the cosmos. He is the world's true Lord. Bow your knee to his lordship. Re-orient every aspect of your life around his rule. He "rules from the cross" for now, but will one day put all his enemies to shame.
- We should heed these verses by guarding the gospel. The gospel can be distorted in many ways. One can add to it, as in the case of the agitators in Galatia. One can assume it, so that before long, you've lost it. Or

---

[19] Simon Gathercole, "The Gospels of Paul and the Kingdom" in *God's Power to Save* (England: Apollos, 2006), 141. Later in the same work he defines the heart of the apostolic gospel as (1) the identity of Jesus as Messiah, (2) his work of atoning sacrifice and justification, and (3) his inauguration of a new dominion, 154. In a talk, I heard Tim Keller summarize these insights as cradle, cross, and crown.

one can take away from it, robbing the Christian of the assurance that Christ has indeed paid for our sin.

- Submit to leadership only if they submit to the gospel. Notice Paul puts his own authority under the authority of the gospel. He says that if *we* preach a different gospel, let us be damned. Follow your leaders. Submit to their leadership (Heb 13:17, 1 Tim 5:17). But keep your eye on the gospel, and when your leaders lose sight of it, let them know and do not follow them. Don't drink the Kool-Aid, no matter how dynamic your preacher's personality is. Know nothing but Christ—that is, Christ crucified (1 Cor 2:2).
- We should also guard our own hearts. The Galatians were *quick* to turn away. Stay close to the cross always. Don't think that you are "just fine." Remain vigilant. Keep a close watch on yourself and your teaching. *"Therefore let anyone who thinks that he stands take heed lest he fall"* (1 Cor 10:12).
- We should also major on the majors. Christians often fight about secondary issues. Churches should *not split* over millennial schemes. The gospel, however, is not secondary. It, not a certain scheme of the future or a fine point of doctrine, should be central. Do you judge other Christians who believe this gospel, but don't see eye to eye with you on some other theological point? Let all theological positions fall into place in light of the glorious truth of Jesus Christ crucified. *He* must remain central.
- Be deeply convinced in your heart that Christ is sufficient. You don't have to add anything to him. It is easy to say this on paper, but where does your mind

go after you sin? Do you run from God, thinking you can't go to him because he is angry with you? Or do you run to him, knowing that you are in Christ, already judged and justified? Jesus is enough!

- Our life's concern should be the glory of God (1:5). We are continually tempted to live for ourselves, or to live to please people (co-dependency), but we should rather follow Paul's example and live to please our great God. In your everyday tasks such as taking out the trash, changing a diaper, putting in another work week, what is your mindset? Let it be to work as unto the Lord, honoring him in all we do.

Chapter 3:
Galatians 1:11-2:14

Passage

For I would have you know, brothers, that the gospel that was preached by me is not man's gospel. For I did not receive it from any man, nor was I taught it, but I received it through a revelation of Jesus Christ. For you have heard of my former life in Judaism, how I persecuted the church of God violently and tried to destroy it. And I was advancing in Judaism beyond many of my own age among my people, so extremely zealous was I for the traditions of my fathers. But when he who had set me apart before I was born, and who called me by his grace, was pleased to reveal his Son to me, in order that I might preach him among the Gentiles, I did not immediately consult with anyone; nor did I go up to Jerusalem to those who were apostles before me, but I went away into Arabia, and returned again to Damascus. Then after three years I went up to Jerusalem to visit Cephas and remained with him fifteen days. But I saw none of the other apostles except James the Lord's brother. (In what I am writing to you, before God, I do not lie!) Then I went into the regions of Syria and Cilicia. And I was still unknown in person to the churches of Judea that are in Christ. They only were hearing it said, "He who used to persecute us is now preaching the faith he once tried to destroy." And they glorified God because of me. Then after fourteen years I went up again to Jerusalem with Barnabas, taking Titus along with me. I went up because of a revelation and set before them (though privately before those who seemed influential) the gospel that I proclaim among the Gentiles, in order to make sure I was not running or had not run in vain. But even Titus, who was with me, was not forced to be circumcised, though he was a Greek. Yet because of false brothers secretly brought in—who slipped in to spy out our freedom that we have in Christ Jesus, so that they might bring us into slavery—to them we did not yield in submission even for a moment, so that the truth of the gospel might be preserved for you. And from those who seemed to be influential (what they were makes no difference to me; God shows no partiality)—those, I say, who seemed influential added nothing to me. On the contrary, when they saw that I had been entrusted with the gospel to the uncircumcised, just as Peter had been entrusted with the gospel to the circumcised (for he who worked through Peter for his apostolic ministry to the circumcised worked also through me for mine to the Gentiles), and when James and Cephas and John, who seemed to be pillars, perceived the grace that was given to me, they gave the right hand of fellowship to Barnabas and me, that we should go to the Gentiles and they to the circumcised. Only, they asked us to remember the poor, the very thing I was eager to do. But when Cephas came to Antioch, I opposed him to his face, because he stood condemned. For before certain men came from James, he was eating with the Gentiles; but when they came he drew back and separated himself, fearing the circumcision party. And the rest of the Jews acted hypocritically along with him, so that even Barnabas was led astray by their hypocrisy. But when I saw that their conduct was not in step with the truth of the gospel, I said to Cephas before them all, "If you, though a Jew, live like a Gentile and not like a Jew, how can you force the Gentiles to live like Jews?"

We are still in the section of the letter where Paul is defending himself. Because this passage recalls several other portions of the New Testament, there will be more Scripture to read, which is always a plus. We are to devote ourselves to the reading of Scripture.

My gospel is not a human gospel (1:11-12)—Main Point

11-12 For I would have you know, brothers, that the gospel that was preached by me is not man's gospel. For I did not receive it from any man, nor was I taught it, but I received it through a revelation of Jesus Christ.

Paul is making the same point here as we saw in verses 1-10: His gospel is not of human origin. No person gave it to him or taught it to him, but he received it from Jesus Christ himself, beginning on the road to Damascus. Consider Acts 9:1-19 (cf. also 22:3-21, 26:12-23):

But Saul, still breathing threats and murder against the disciples of the Lord, went to the high priest and asked him for letters to the synagogues at Damascus, so that if he found any belonging to the Way, men or women, he might bring them bound to Jerusalem. Now as he went on his way, he approached Damascus, and suddenly a light from heaven flashed around him. And falling to the ground he heard a voice saying to him, "Saul, Saul, why are you persecuting me?" And he said, "Who are you, Lord?" And he said, "I am Jesus, whom you are persecuting. But rise and enter the city, and you will be told what you are to do." The men who were traveling with him stood speechless, hearing the voice but seeing no one. Saul rose from the ground, and although his eyes were opened, he saw nothing. So they led him by the hand and brought him into Damascus. And for three days he was without sight, and neither ate nor drank. Now there was a disciple at Damascus named Ananias. The Lord said to him in a vision, "Ananias." And he said, "Here I am, Lord." And the Lord said to him, "Rise and go to the street called Straight, and at the house of Judas look for a man of Tarsus named Saul, for behold, he is praying, and he has seen in a vision a man named Ananias come in and lay his hands on him so that he might regain his sight." But Ananias answered, "Lord, I have heard from many about this man, how much evil he has done to your saints at Jerusalem. And here he has authority from the chief priests to bind all who call on your name." But the Lord said to him, "Go, for he is a chosen instrument of mine to carry my name before the Gentiles and kings and the children of Israel. For I will show him how much he must suffer for the sake of my name." So Ananias departed and entered the house. And laying his hands on him he said, "Brother Saul, the Lord Jesus who appeared to you on the road by which you came has sent me so that you may regain your sight and be filled with the Holy Spirit." And immediately something like scales fell from his eyes, and he regained his sight. Then he rose and was baptized; and taking food, he was strengthened. For some days he was with the disciples at Damascus.

Supporting Evidence (1:13-2:14)

13-14 *For you have heard of my former life in Judaism, how I persecuted the church of God violently and tried to destroy it. And I was advancing in Judaism beyond many of my own age among my people, so extremely zealous was I for the traditions of my fathers.*

Paul shows that his past hostility is evidence that his gospel is not man-made. He formerly persecuted the church of God. It is *God's* church, which shows the frightfulness of his former activity. It also shows that there is a distinction being made here. The people of Israel (Judaism) are no longer the Lord's assembly (*ecclēsia*). Now Christians are the Lord's people. This community (*i.e.*, the church) is the end-time equivalent to the Old Testament assembly (*kahal YHWH*—Deut 23:1-3, 8, 1 Chron 28:8, Mic 2:5, Neh 13:1).

Paul was advancing beyond his fellow Jewish peers. In other words, his future was bright. From Philippians we learn that Paul had more reason to boast in the flesh than his peers. He was circumcised on the eighth day in accordance with the law, of the people of Israel, of the tribe of Benjamin, a Hebrew of Hebrews, as to the law a Pharisee, as to zeal a persecutor of the church, as to righteousness under the law, blameless (Phil 3:4-6). He had no earthly reason to leave Judaism. He clearly had it made. In other words, his current zeal for the Messiah is obviously not a result of human deliberation.

Paul says he was very *zealous* (*zēlōtēs*) for the traditions of his fathers. By using the term *zealous,* he is almost certainly alluding to the commended zeal of Phinehas in Numbers 25:1-13. Do you remember the story?

> *While Israel lived in Shittim, the people began to whore with the daughters of Moab. These invited the people to the sacrifices of their gods, and the people ate and bowed down to their gods. So Israel yoked himself to Baal of Peor. And the anger of the LORD was kindled against Israel. And the LORD said to Moses, "Take all the chiefs of the people and hang them in the sun before the LORD, that the fierce anger of the LORD may turn away from Israel." And Moses said to the judges of Israel, "Each of you kill those of his men who have yoked themselves to Baal of Peor." And behold, one of the people of Israel came and brought a Midianite woman to his family, in the sight of Moses and in the sight of the whole congregation of the people of Israel, while they were weeping in the entrance of the tent of meeting. When Phinehas the son of Eleazar, son of Aaron the priest, saw it, he rose and left the congregation and took a spear in his hand and went after the man of Israel into the chamber and pierced both of them, the man of Israel and the woman through her belly. Thus the plague on the people of Israel was stopped. Nevertheless, those who died by the plague were twenty-four thousand. And the LORD said to Moses, "Phinehas the son of Eleazar, son of Aaron the priest, has turned back my wrath from the people of Israel, in that he was jealous (zēloō) with my jealousy (zēlos) among them, so that I did not consume the people of Israel in my jealousy (zēlos). Therefore say, 'Behold, I give to him my covenant of peace, and it shall be to him and to his descendants after him the covenant of a perpetual priesthood, because he was jealous (zēloō) for his God and made atonement for the people of Israel.*

Paul was continuing in the tradition of Phinehas, zealous for the traditions of his fathers.

15-17 *But when he who had set me apart before I was born, and who called me by his grace, was pleased to reveal his Son to me, in order that I might preach him among the Gentiles, I did not immediately consult with anyone; nor did I go up to Jerusalem to those who were apostles before me, but I went away into Arabia, and returned again to Damascus.*

Paul's gospel is not man-made; rather he was called by God. God has a sovereign purpose and his purpose will be done (Eph 1:11). He needed a man who had a keen mind, soaked in the Hebrew Scriptures, so he raised up a Saul whom he would turn to a Paul. Paul likens his ministry to the ministry of the prophets. Paul said that he was set apart before he was born. Similarly, Jeremiah 1:5 says, "Before I formed you in the womb I knew you, before you were born I set you apart; I appointed you as a prophet to the nations" (cf. also Isa 49:1).

God called him and revealed Christ to him, and did so for a purpose: so Paul would preach Jesus among the Gentiles. He was called and commissioned.[20] When God did this, Paul didn't go and consult anyone. He is still showing that he is not dependent upon anyone for his gospel, Jerusalem apostles included.

18-22 *Then after three years I went up to Jerusalem to visit Cephas and remained with him fifteen days. But I saw none of the other apostles except James the Lord's brother. (In what I am writing to you, before God, I do not lie!) Then I went into the regions of Syria and Cilicia. And I was still unknown in person to the churches of Judea that are in Christ.*

---

[20] Gorman, *Cruciformity*, 28.

Paul shows that he is independent by noting his obscurity in Judea. He didn't go to see Peter until three years later. Add to that, he was only with him fifteen days. Paul wasn't dependent on the apostles for his gospel, but on Jesus Christ.

Notice how Paul refers to the churches in Judea in Galatians 1:22: they are "in Christ." Jesus is our representative. All the blessings of salvation are found *in him*.[21] Paul uses this corporate language in other places in this letter as well:

> 2:4 *Yet because of false brothers secretly brought in—who slipped in to spy out our freedom that we have* ***in Christ Jesus,*** *so that they might bring us into slavery—*
>
> 2:17 *But if, in our endeavor to be justified* ***in Christ,*** *we too were found to be sinners, is Christ then a servant of sin? Certainly not!*
>
> 2:20 *I have been crucified* ***with Christ***
>
> 3:26 *for* ***in Christ Jesus*** *you are all sons of God, through faith.*
>
> 3:28 *There is neither Jew nor Greek, there is neither slave nor free, there is neither male nor female, for you are all one* ***in Christ Jesus.*** (emphasis mine)

Through faith, we are transferred from the kingdom of darkness to the kingdom of Christ. We are now "in Christ" not "in Adam." Herman Ridderbos writes, "Christ is the second Adam, in whom the believers are incorporated in the sense that they belong to the new order of life and of

---

[21] John Murray, *Redemption Accomplished and Applied* (Grand Rapids: Eerdmans, 1955), 161-174; Richard Gaffin, *By Faith, Not by Sight* (Waynesboro, GA: Paternoster, 2006), 36.

grace as distinguished from the order represented by the first Adam."[22]

As a side note, Galatians 1:19 says that Jesus had a brother, James. Contrary to the Roman Catholic Church, Mary must not have remained a virgin after all.

23-24 *They only were hearing it said, "He who used to persecute us is now preaching the faith he once tried to destroy." And they glorified God because of me.*

Paul had relatively little contact with the apostles and the churches in Judea. They were only *hearing*—not talking or seeing. Acts 8:1-3 says, "And Saul approved of his execution. And there arose on that day a great persecution against the church in Jerusalem, and they were all scattered throughout the regions of Judea and Samaria, except the apostles. Devout men buried Stephen and made great lamentation over him. But Saul was ravaging the church, and entering house after house, he dragged off men and women and committed them to prison." Acts 9:1 says Saul was breathing out threats to murder the Lord's disciples. Paul uses "the faith" here to refer to a body of teaching. Paul went from a persecutor of the faith to a persecuted advocate of it.[23] There had been a clear and decisive conversion, and this caused them to glorify God because of his work in Saul's life.

The Jerusalem leaders recognized his authority (2:1-10)

1 *Then after fourteen years I went up again to Jerusalem with Barnabas, taking Titus along with me.*

---

[22] Ridderbos, *Galatians,* 72 n.4.

[23] Gorman, *Cruciformity,* 27.

He didn't go back to Jerusalem for 14 years (Acts 11:27). He is still showing the independence of his gospel.

> 2 *I went up because of a revelation and set before them (though privately before those who seemed influential) the gospel that I proclaim among the Gentiles, in order to make sure I was not running or had not run in vain.*

When saying "those who seemed to be influential" he is probably taking a phrase the agitators frequently used since it is repeated a couple of times. They were playing up the Jerusalem leaders against his leadership. It is not that Paul really believed that he could have been wrong about the gospel, but if the gospel he proclaimed contradicted their gospel, from a practical perspective, there would be all kinds of trouble. His ministry would be constantly undermined because people would follow everywhere he went to discount the message he preached.

> 3 *But even Titus, who was with me, was not forced to be circumcised, though he was a Greek.*

Titus, a Gentile, went to Jerusalem and was not compelled to be circumcised. A question that rightly comes to mind is, "Why did Paul circumcise Timothy?" (Acts 16:3). What was the difference between Titus and Timothy? With Timothy, it would be an aid to evangelism in the synagogues, so he did it. Paul was willing and able to be flexible in order to win converts. In 1 Corinthians 9:19-23, he writes, "For though I am free from all, I have made myself a servant to all, that I might win more of them. To the Jews I became as a Jew, in order to win Jews. To those under the law I became as one under the law (though not being myself under the law) that I might win those under the law. To those outside the law I became as one outside the law (not being outside the law of God but under the law of Christ) that I might win those outside the law. To the weak I became weak, that I might win the weak. I have become all things to all people, that by all means I might save some. I do it all for the sake of the gospel, that I may share with them in its blessings."

With Titus however, people were insisting that to be justified, you had to believe and be circumcised. So if Titus was circumcised, it would look as if Jesus were insufficient. May it never be! The differences between the situations of Titus and Timothy with regard to circumcision are night and day. Paul was not a relativist, but one who deeply adored the sufficiency of Jesus Christ.[24]

> 4-5 *Yet because of false brothers secretly brought in—who slipped in to spy out our freedom that we have in Christ Jesus, so*

---

[24] D. A. Carson and Douglas Moo write, "To circumcise Timothy and to refuse to circumcise Titus, for instance, was certainly inconsistent at the level of mere performance. But from Paul's perspective, both actions were deeply principled. He refused to permit Titus to be circumcised in a Christian context where circumcision would have signaled that Titus (and Paul, too) agreed that one needed to be a proper Jew to accept the Jewish Messiah—and that would have jeopardized the exclusive sufficiency of Christ. In the context of Jewish synagogue, however, where Paul was resolutely trying to win people to Christ and no one was reading in any Christological implications, the circumcision of Timothy was merely part and parcel of his willingness to 'become all things to all people so that by all possible means [he] might save some' (1 Cor 9:22)," in *An Introduction to the New Testament* 2nd ed. (Grand Rapids: Zondervan, 2005), 468 n.31.

that they might bring us into slavery— to them we did not yield in submission even for a moment, so that the truth of the gospel might be preserved for you.

Paul calls them false brothers and claims that their motives are evil. Like spies who infiltrate an enemy camp, pretending to be friendly toward them to strategically learn their enemy's situation, they slipped in to spy on their freedom in Christ and make them slaves to the law. This should warn us that at times, unbelievers will enter the church to seek to distort the gospel. We must always be on guard. But they didn't submit for a moment so that the truth of the gospel would be preserved. Part of the truth of the gospel is that we are no longer under the old covenant law. We are freed from the law through Christ. Isn't it incredible that Paul equates following the law with slavery? This shows just how different the Christian view of the law is as opposed to the Jewish view. Christ has accomplished the new exodus, releasing us from the slavery of the old covenant.

6-10 *And from those who seemed to be influential (what they were makes no difference to me; God shows no partiality)—those, I say, who seemed influential added nothing to me. On the contrary, when they saw that I had been entrusted with the gospel to the uncircumcised, just as Peter had been entrusted with the gospel to the circumcised (for he who worked through Peter for his apostolic ministry to the circumcised worked also through me for mine to the Gentiles), and when James and Cephas and John, who seemed to be pillars, perceived the grace that was given to me, they gave the right hand of fellowship to Barnabas and me, that we should go to the Gentiles and they to the circumcised. Only, they asked us to remember the poor, the very thing I was eager to do.*

The end of verse six is a significant point. Why didn't they add anything? Because they *saw* that Paul had been entrusted with the gospel (Gal 2:7a) and *recognized* the grace that was given to Paul (Gal 2:9a). Paul and Barnabas were given the right hand of fellowship by the Jerusalem apostles. They preached the *same* gospel. All the apostles agreed. The Jerusalem apostles only asked that they remember the poor in Jerusalem as they went to the Gentiles. Simon Gathercole writes, "Paul's concern for the poor as evidenced here is in accord with the broader principle demonstrated throughout Scripture that genuine preaching of the gospel in every age must be accompanied by the meeting of physical needs as well, just as Jesus healed the sick and cast out demons along with his preaching ministry."[25]

Paul Even Rebukes Peter (2:11-14)

Here we have the famous apostolic dispute. Some church fathers said that they were play-acting and not really disagreeing but wanting to address certain issues. Likewise, the Roman Catholic Church says the apostles arranged the dispute. Clement said it was a different Cephas, and not really the apostle Peter. Augustine got it right, however. He knew that truth trumps office. Peter and Paul didn't disagree about the gospel but about Peter's behavior.

---

[25] Simon Gathercole, "Galatians" in *The ESV Study Bible,* (Wheaton, IL: Crossway, 2008) 2247. See chapter four in Tim Chester and Steve Timmis, *Total Church* (Wheaton, IL: Crossway, 2008).

As an aside, there are many out there who claim that Christianity is a man-made religion. But if Christianity were a man-made religion, do you think they would have included a dispute between two key leaders in their holy writings? Doubtful. It would have been smarter to leave this account out. Paul brings up the episode to further show the truth and independence of his gospel. He was bold enough to confront even Peter.

> 12-13 *For before certain men came from James, he was eating with the Gentiles; but when they came he drew back and separated himself, fearing the circumcision party. And the rest of the Jews acted hypocritically along with him, so that even Barnabas was led astray by their hypocrisy.*

Peter was eating with Gentiles and was eating unclean foods (Deut 14:21, Lev 11), as was his new custom. Peter did not pack his kosher lunch but was eating with the Gentiles, which meant the clean laws of the old covenant were no longer operative. Peter knew this well. Do you recall the vision given to Peter in Acts 10-11? Consider Acts 11:1-18:

> *Now the apostles and the brothers who were throughout Judea heard that the Gentiles also had received the word of God. So when Peter went up to Jerusalem, the circumcision party criticized him, saying, "You went to uncircumcised men and ate with them." But Peter began and explained it to them in order: "I was in the city of Joppa praying, and in a trance I saw a vision, something like a great sheet descending, being let down from heaven by its four corners, and it came down to me. Looking at it closely, I observed animals and beasts of prey and reptiles and birds of the air. And I heard a voice saying to me, 'Rise, Peter; kill and eat.' But I said, 'By no means, Lord; for nothing common or unclean has ever entered my mouth.' But the voice answered a second time from heaven, 'What God has made clean, do not call common.' This happened three times, and all was drawn up again into heaven. And behold, at that*

> *very moment three men arrived at the house in which we were, sent to me from Caesarea. And the Spirit told me to go with them, making no distinction. These six brothers also accompanied me, and we entered the man's house. And he told us how he had seen the angel stand in his house and say, 'Send to Joppa and bring Simon who is called Peter; he will declare to you a message by which you will be saved, you and all your household.' As I began to speak, the Holy Spirit fell on them just as on us at the beginning. And I remembered the word of the Lord, how he said, 'John baptized with water, but you will be baptized with the Holy Spirit.' If then God gave the same gift to them as he gave to us when we believed in the Lord Jesus Christ, who was I that I could stand in God's way?" When they heard these things they fell silent. And they glorified God, saying, "Then to the Gentiles also God has granted repentance that leads to life."*

So theologically, Peter and Paul were on the same team. Peter knew better than to act the way he did, but in a moment of pressure, he acted in confusion, not realizing the dire consequences of his actions.

Who are the circumcision party? They could be Judaizers within the church, normal Jewish Christians, or simply Jews. The Bible uses that phrase to refer to all three, but it makes the most sense in the context to take them as unbelieving Jews. The "men from James" were not the same group as "the circumcision party." Peter would not have been afraid of James' men since they were on the same team. The "men from James" weren't simply from Jerusalem, but from James himself. Men from James came and warned Peter that Jewish Christians in Jerusalem were being persecuted because of his behavior. Men from James came and warned of the "circumcision group." They may have said, "Be careful Peter. Things are tense here, and many of our people are losing everything. Don't make it worse for them by openly disregarding our customs." Peter was probably overly concerned for his fellow Jerusalem Christians, and failed to thoroughly think through the implications of his "caution."[26] Even Barnabas, who had helped found Gentile churches, was led astray as well. The poor Gentile Christians at the table must have felt like second-rate believers.

> **14** *But when I saw that their conduct was not in step with the truth of the gospel, I said to Cephas before them all, "If you, though a Jew, live like a Gentile and not like a Jew, how can you force the Gentiles to live like Jews?"*

Their conduct was not in line with the truth of the gospel. They were acting like the false brothers who were distorting the gospel. We know this by the language Paul uses. Here, in Galatians 2:14, he asks Peter how he can force (*anankazō*) the Gentiles to Judaize (*i.e.*, live like a Jew). This is the same verb that Paul used earlier in Galatians 2:3 when he said that Titus was not forced (*anankazō*) to be circumcised. Also, he uses the phrase "truth of the gospel" here in Galatians 2:14 and in 2:5 (cf. Gal 5:7). In Galatians 2:5, he resisted the false brothers to preserve the "truth of the gospel" (*hē alētheia tou euangeliou*). In Galatians 2:14, he condemns Peter for not keeping in step with the "truth of the gospel" (*tēn alētheian tou euangeliou*). Paul is warning Peter not to be like the false brothers. The word for "conduct not in step" is *orthopodousin*, from which we get our

---

[26] I owe this recreation of the scenario to D.A. Carson, whom I affectionately call "The Evangelical Pope."

word *orthopedics*. Peter's feet were crooked and Paul is calling him to get straight with the gospel.

Application

- Our gospel is from God (1:11-12). It is not man-made. It's a word from above. It is authoritative and true. We can have confidence in it. We can and should bank our eternity on it. If you reject the gospel, you reject the one who is giving you your every breath.
- Even amidst the rebuke, Paul still calls the Galatians "brothers" (1:11). He is calling his brothers and sisters back. Are there people in your life who have professed faith but are now straying? Call them back to repentance with the gospel. God uses his people to restore straying saints (Gal 6:1, Matt 18:15-18). One of my best friends is a guy we call Cheese (short for Cheeseburger). He was very zealous for Christ, but began to walk away from the Lord after his engagement to his *fiancē* was broken off. Another friend and I refused to let him go. We would call every couple of weeks and leave messages on his phone. Of course, he would avoid our calls, but we just kept telling him that we loved him and that he knew better and needed to repent. Eventually, the Lord answered our prayers and used our love to bring Cheese to repentance. He is now in seminary training for ministry. I currently have another friend who is straying as well. I text him or—providentially—just as I type this, he sent me a text message asking if our son Josiah was born yet. He was born three months ago, but I praise God that now this friend is initiating communication with me, even if it is small. I was about to write that I simply

text him or send him an occasional email to let him know I am praying for him and am here for him. Don't write them off, but pursue them with love and prayer.

- Paul's conversion was dramatic (1:13-15). Paul speaks of his former way of life. Then come the all-important words "But God" (1:15). Only sovereign grace can explain Saul to Paul. Grace is powerful and transforming. Do you believe that?
- Don't give up on your unbelieving friends and family. No doubt, most people held out no hope for Saul. They had a small view of God's grace. Again, God's sovereign grace is powerful. Continue to be faithful in evangelism and prayer.
- Notice the response of those who heard about Paul's conversion: they glorified God. We should emulate this. Often in our circles, conversions are doubted. We hear about a brother or sister coming to faith and say "Halleluiah," but are inwardly thinking, "Let's see if the seed takes root." While this attitude isn't completely wrong, we should praise God when people come to Christ, and not be too skeptical.
- What can you change in your life that would make others glorify God because of you (1:24)?
- Notice that to impose the law-covenant is slavery (2:4). Devotion to the law results in bondage. Legalism is so dangerous. As the hymn says,

  "Lay your deadly 'doing' down
  Down at Jesus' feet.

Stand in him, in him alone
Gloriously Complete."[27]

- If we add to the gospel (even in actions) we stand condemned. Be on guard always.
- Remember the poor (2:10). We find this throughout the Bible. God cares for the poor. Read the gospel of Luke sometime, taking note of how often the poor and economic issues are mentioned. Remember that life does not consist in an abundance of things. Make sure that your brothers and sisters in Christ are taken care of. We will see more of this in chapter six.
- Public sin needs a public rebuke (2:11). Paul did not follow Jesus' teaching in Matthew 18:15-18. Sometimes, sin is so serious and severe that it must be dealt with immediately. Peter's sin had serious public consequences, so Paul had to deal with it immediately and publicly. The truth of the gospel was at stake.
- Like Peter, accept correction humbly. Although not in this text, we do know that Peter received Paul's rebuke and did begin to walk in line with the truth of the gospel. Part of the message of the gospel is that we are sinners who have done wrong. So don't get all upset when confronted. Use your critics as coaches. Learn from them. Learn which part is true. Admit that you are often wrong and need God's forgiveness daily.

---

[27] I do not want readers to think that "mere belief" is all that is required. We are going to see in chapters five and six that there are many ways we are called to act. Faith works through love (Gal 5:6).

- Even those who know the gospel are capable of hypocrisy. "Even Barnabas"who had defended Paul, acted in hypocrisy. How is hypocrisy at odds with the truth of the gospel? Again, part of the message of the gospel is that you are a sinner. Don't act like you are not. Don't act like you are not in desperate need of the cross of Christ. You are. Are you a different person at home than you are at church? Oh, how important it is to live consistently in front of our families. Stay close to the cross and guard your life. Keep in step with the truth of the gospel.
- Peter was not keeping in step with the truth of the gospel. In this context, that means he was *acting* as if Jews and Gentiles did not stand on equal ground. The gospel has a vast number of implications for all of life. We must seek to align all aspects of our life so that we walk in line with the truth of the gospel. The Christian life is a continual realignment process. How can we make the same mistake Peter did? How do we fail to "eat" with other Christians? We can "refuse to eat" with people of a different race, political persuasion, minor theological difference, or lower social status. The tendency of the heart is to feel superior to the group that is unlike you—so you are clean and they are unclean—but the gospel says we are all unclean, and all clean in Christ. Tim Keller writes, "Paul is showing that we never 'get beyond the gospel' in our Christian life to something more 'advanced.' It is not just the A-B-C's but the A to Z of Christianity. The gospel is not just the minimum required doctrine for entrance into the kingdom, but the way we make all of

our progress in the kingdom. We are not made right with God through faith in the gospel and then sanctified and matured through mere moral effort. Faith in the gospel is *also* the way to grow (Gal3:1-3; Col 1:3-6). It is common to think, 'The gospel is for non-Christians. But once we are saved, we grow through work and obedience.' But work that is not 'in line' with the gospel will not sanctify — it will strangle. All our problems come from a failure to apply the gospel. The gospel changes every area of our lives."[28]

- Finally, keep in mind that your behavior affects others. Because of Peter's hypocrisy, Barnabas was led astray. Parents, your behavior affects your children. Husbands, your behavior affects your wives and vice versa. Friend, your walk will affect your friend. Sibling, your life will affect your sibling.

[28] Tim Keller, *Galatians* (New York: Redeemer Presbyterian Church, 2003), 53.

Chapter 4: Galatians 2:15-3:5

Passage

We ourselves are Jews by birth and not Gentile sinners; yet we know that a person is not justified by works of the law but through faith in Jesus Christ, so we also have believed in Christ Jesus, in order to be justified by faith in Christ and not by works of the law, because by works of the law no one will be justified. But if, in our endeavor to be justified in Christ, we too were found to be sinners, is Christ then a servant of sin? Certainly not! For if I rebuild what I tore down, I prove myself to be a transgressor. For through the law I died to the law, so that I might live to God. I have been crucified with Christ. It is no longer I who live, but Christ who lives in me. And the life I now live in the flesh I live by faith in the Son of God, who loved me and gave himself for me. I do not nullify the grace of God, for if justification were through the law, then Christ died for no purpose. O foolish Galatians! Who has bewitched you? It was before your eyes that Jesus Christ was publicly portrayed as crucified. Let me ask you only this: Did you receive the Spirit by works of the law or by hearing with faith? Are you so foolish? Having begun by the Spirit, are you now being perfected by the flesh? Did you suffer so many things in vain—if indeed it was in vain? Does he who supplies the Spirit to you and works miracles among you do so by works of the law, or by hearing with faith—

We will now finish up the section of Paul's self-defense and begin Paul's theological defense (which starts in chapter three).

The nature of the gospel (2:15-21)

Galatians 2:15-21 provides the reason given for Galatians 2:14. This section is probably a transition from what he said to Peter, to what he wants the Galatians to hear directly, since the whole incident is brought up to illustrate the point Paul is making: he is not dependent on anyone and has not distorted the gospel. In summary form, these verses lay out the gospel Paul preached.

> 15-16 *We ourselves are Jews by birth and not Gentile sinners; yet we know that a person is not justified by works of the law but through faith in Jesus Christ, so we also have believed in Christ Jesus, in order to be justified by faith in Christ and not by works of the law, because by works of the law no one will be justified.*

Peter should know, even though he is a Jew and not a "filthy Gentile," that no one is justified by works of the law but by faith in Christ.[29] In Galatians 2:16 he uses the word *person* (*anthrōpos*) to show Peter that at the end of the day—all people, Jew or Gentile—are in the same boat: persons in need of grace.

The doctrine of justification has become a hot topic recently, particularly in New Testament studies.[30] Briefly, justification is not an infusion of righteousness. It is not *simply* becoming a member of the covenant community. The verb *justify* (*dikaioō*) occurs eight times in Galatians:[31] three times in 2:16 and:

---

[29] The identification of Gentiles and sinners was a standard Jewish axiom (1 Sam 15:18, Ps 9:18 LXX, SS 2:1-2, 17:25, Job 23:23-24, 24:28, 4 Ezra 3:28-36, Matt 5:47, 26:45. See Barclay, *Obeying the Truth*, 77 n.7).

[30] Probably the best one volume treatment of the issues is Stephen Westerholm's *Perspectices Old and New on Paul* (Grand Rapids: Eerdmans, 2004).

[31] Schreiner, *Galatians*, 118.

> 2:17 *But if, in our endeavor to be justified in Christ, we too were found to be sinners, is Christ then a servant of sin? Certainly not!*
>
> 3:8 *And the Scripture, foreseeing that God would justify the Gentiles by faith, preached the gospel beforehand to Abraham, saying, "In you shall all the nations be blessed."*
>
> 3:11 *Now it is evident that no one is justified before God by the law, for "The righteous shall live by faith."*
>
> 3:24 *So then, the law was our guardian until Christ came, in order that we might be justified by faith.*
>
> 5:4 *You are severed from Christ, you who would be justified by the law; you have fallen away from grace.*

The opposite of justification is condemnation. To justify is to declare righteous.[32] "The verb *justify* refers to God's verdict of not-guilty on the day of judgment (Rom 2:13). God's eschatological verdict has now been announced in advance for those who believe in Jesus Christ."[33] Justification is linked with forgiveness of sins, as Romans 4:5-8 shows:

> *And to the one who does not work but trusts him who justifies the ungodly, his faith is counted as righteousness, just as David also speaks of the blessing of the one to whom God counts righteousness apart from works: "Blessed are those whose lawless deeds are forgiven, and whose sins are covered; blessed is the man against whom the Lord will not count his sin.*

Tied to the justification debates is the meaning of the phrase "works of the law." "Law" (*nomos*) in Paul's writing

---

[32] Westerholm, *Perspectives,* 286.

[33] Schreiner, *Galatians,* 118.

almost always refers to the Mosaic covenant.[34] There are a few exceptions where he seems to use the word as a principle or something similar, but the vast majority refers to the Mosaic law-covenant. "Works of law" does not mean legalism, or simply Jewish boundary-markers, but rather all that the law commands.

There has also been a stormy debate on how to translate *pisteōs Iēsou Christou.* Should it be translated "faith in Christ" (objective genitive) or "faithfulness of Christ" (subjective genitive)? The arguments for the subjective genitive are strong.[35] The phrase occurs twice here in Galatians 2:16. It also occurs in:

- Galations 3:22: *But the Scripture imprisoned everything under sin, so that the promise by faith in Jesus Christ might be given to those who believe.*
- Romans 3:22: *the righteousness of God through faith in Jesus Christ for all who believe.*
- Romans 3:26: *It was to show his righteousness at the present time, so that he might be just and the justifier of the one who has faith in Jesus (of the one who lives because of Jesus' faithfulness)*
- Ephesians 3:12: *in whom we have boldness and access with confidence through our faith in him (through his faithfulness),*

---

[34] N.T. Wright, *Justification* (Downers Grove, IL: IVP Academic, 2009), 116. See Douglas J. Moo, "'Law,' 'Works of the Law,' and Legalism in Paul," *Westminster Theological Journal* 45, no. 1 (Spring 1983): 90-99; idem, "Paul and the Law in the Last Ten Years," *Scottish Journal of Theology* 40 (1987):287-307.

[35] See Richard Hays, *The Faith of Jesus Christ* (Grand Rapids: Eerdmans, 1983).

- Philippians 3:9: *and be found in him, not having a righteousness of my own that comes from the law, but that which comes through faith in Christ, the righteousness from God that depends on faith*

Also, Romans 3:3 has the same construction with *theos* (God) in the genitive (*tēn pistein tou theou)* meaning the faithfulness *of God,* not faith in God. Also, in Romans 3:22, Galatians 2:16, and Philippians 3:9, faith in Christ is superfluous, as believing is also mentioned in these passages. This interpretation also makes better sense of Galatians 3:23 and 3:25 where Paul speaks of "faith" in a redemptive historical manner.[36] So Paul could be laying out both the objective and subjective bases of the gospel: the faithfulness of Jesus and the necessity of human faith.

On the other hand, the reason Paul mentions belief and faith together is not superfluous but *emphatic*. Righteousness is available to *all* now in the new age, apart from law, whether Jew or Gentile—through faith! Also, Paul often contrasts human works with human faith (both human activities). The objective genitive reading also makes most sense in the context. Consider Galatians 3:7, which is an inference of Galatians 3:6. Galatians 3:6 says to consider Abraham who believed God and it was counted to him as righteousness. Verse seven then says, "Therefore, know then that it is those of faith (*i.e.*, believers) who are the children of Abraham. Taking verse seven as "those of the faithfulness (implied: of Jesus) does not do justice to the inference in verse seven, where it is clearly referring to human

---

36 Schreiner, *Galatians*, 127.

faith.[37] Although the arguments are strong for the subjective reading, and nothing is lost theologically, I still tend to think that Paul is emphasizing the need for human faith, regardless of one's ethnicity.[38]

Here Paul gives two reasons to believe in Christ in verse 16: in order to be justified, and because no-one is justified by works (see Ps 143:2). Literally, by the works of the law all flesh *will not* be justified.

> 17 *But if, in our endeavor to be justified in Christ, we too were found to be sinners, is Christ then a servant of sin? Certainly not!*

So does becoming a Christian make you a sinner because you are not following the old covenant law, making Christ a servant of sin? No way! Also notice that we are justified "in Christ." In another place, Paul similarly writes that he desires to be found "in Christ," not having a righteousness of his own from the law, but that which comes from God through faith in Christ (Phil 3:9). Justification, and indeed all salvific blessings, flows from our union with the Messiah.[39]

> 18 *For if I rebuild what I tore down, I prove myself to be a transgressor.*

Paul now shifts to "I" to speak representatively. He already "tore down" the law, so if he set it back up, he would be a transgressor(*i.e.*, one who breaks the law). With the resurrection of Jesus, the old covenant is no longer our authority, so to re-establish it is to go against God's will and

---

[37] Ibid., 157.

[38] Barclay, *Obeying the Truth*, 78 n.8.

[39] Westerholm's *Perspectives New and Old* misses this key theme.

be a transgressor. New Testament scholar Richard Longenecker writes, "So here in v 18 Paul insists that to revert to the Mosaic law as a Christian is what really constitutes breaking the law, for then the law's true intent is nullified."[40]

> 19 *For through the law I died to the law, so that I might live to God.*

The Commandments brought death.[41] Paul uses similar reasoning in Romans 7:1-6:

> *Or do you not know, brothers—for I am speaking to those who know the law—that the law is binding on a person only as long as he lives? Thus a married woman is bound by law to her husband while he lives, but if her husband dies she is released from the law of marriage. Accordingly, she will be called an adulteress if she lives with another man while her husband is alive. But if her husband dies, she is free from that law, and if she marries another man she is not an adulteress. Likewise, my brothers, you also have died to the law through the body of Christ, so that you may belong to another, to him who has been raised from the dead, in order that we may bear fruit for God. For while we were living in the flesh, our sinful passions, aroused by the law, were at work in our members to bear fruit for death. But now we are released from the law, having died to that*

---

[40] Longenecker, *Galatians,* 91. Mark Seifrid writes, "To re-establish a relationship to the law after having believed in Christ is to violate the law itself. The one who returns to the law is a transgressor of it," in *Christ, Our Righteousness* (Downers Grove: IVP, 2000), 107. Paul may mean that he will be a transgressor of the law of Christ, which he will bring up in Galatians 6:2.

[41] See Westherholm, *Perspectives,* 297-340; Seifrid, *Christ, Our Righteousness,* 95-128.

which held us captive, so that we serve not under the old written code but in the new life of the Spirit.

"The letter kills but the Spirit brings life" (2 Cor 3:6). The law could not bring life (Gal 3:21). Romans 7:9 says, "I was once alive apart from the law, but when the commandment came, sin came alive and I died." The law cannot give what it demands. So we die through the law. The new age is here and hence we are not under law.

20 *I have been crucified with Christ. It is no longer I who live, but Christ who lives in me. And the life I now live in the flesh I live by faith in the Son of God, who loved me and gave himself for me.*

How can we have been crucified with Christ? The crucifixion is the center of history (BC/AD). He is our representative. When he died, we died. Again, we gain insight by considering Paul's similar teaching in Romans 6:1-8:

What shall we say then? Are we to continue in sin that grace may abound? By no means! How can we who died to sin still live in it? Do you not know that all of us who have been baptized into Christ Jesus were baptized into his death? We were buried therefore with him by baptism into death, in order that, just as Christ was raised from the dead by the glory of the Father, we too might walk in newness of life. For if we have been united with him in a death like his, we shall certainly be united with him in a resurrection like his. We know that our old self was crucified with him in order that the body of sin might be brought to nothing, so that we would no longer be enslaved to sin. For one who has died has been set free from sin. Now if we have died with Christ, we believe that we will also live with him.

Our old person, who we were in Adam, no longer lives. That person is dead.[42] We see this truth taught by Paul elsewhere:

> Ephesians 4:20-24: *But that is not the way you learned Christ!—assuming that you have heard about him and were taught in him, as the truth is in Jesus, to put off your old self, which belongs to your former manner of life and is corrupt through deceitful desires, and to be renewed in the spirit of your minds, and to put on the new self, created after the likeness of God in true righteousness and holiness.*

> Colossians 3:9: *Do not lie to one another, seeing that you have put off the old self with its practices*

Again and again, we have seen that the new age has come. The last Adam has died and killed the old Adam. To insist on the old covenant law is to insist on returning to the present evil age (Gal 1:4). They were confused about what time it was in redemptive history.

Jesus is the Son who loves by giving.[43] Many today rightly criticize our postmodern culture for being overly individualistic. This is, of course, true, but let's not throw the baby out with the bathwater. Some today are over-reacting to contemporary culture and teaching that the Bible only gives us corporate structures. But listen to Paul in this pas-

---

[42] Michael Gorman writes, "Paul says that he himself has been crucified with Christ and no longer lives (Gal 2:19-20). That is, he no longer lives for himself and the desires inspired by the flesh, just as he no longer lives for sin or the world. Rather, he lives for God, he lives for Christ," *Cruciformity,* 126.

[43] Michael Gorman translates this phrase, "the Son of God, who loved me by giving himself for me," *Cruciformity,* 219.

sage. The God of Scripture loves the individual! Jesus loved *me* and gave himself for *me*! "Son" is of course a Messianic title. God promised David that he would give him a son, and would establish his throne and give him an everlasting kingdom (2 Sam 7). Jesus is the promised Davidic Son. This Christ now lives in me. Thomas Schreiner writes, "The indwelling of Christ signifies the arrival of the new age of redemptive history, the fulfillment of God's saving promises."[44]

> 21 *I do not nullify the grace of God, for if justification were through the law, then Christ died for no purpose.*

Christ will do everything for you or he will do nothing for you.

The Judaizers did not see the necessity and sufficiency of Christ. They were nullifying the grace of God. Here in this verse we have a sentence summary of the argument. John Chrysostom writes, "Christ's death is a plain proof of the inability of the law to justify us. And if it does justify, then His death is superfluous."[45] I hope the message is clear thus far: the law cannot bring a right standing with God. Roger Nicole tells a story to illustrate the point:

> If your house was burning down but your whole family escaped, and I came to you and said, "Let me show you how much I love you!" and ran into the fiery house and

---

[44] Schreiner, *Galatians,* 136.

[45] John Chrysostom, "Galatians," in "Chrysostom: Homilies on Galatians, Ephesians, Philippians, Colossians, Thessalonians, Timothy, Titus, and Philemon," in *Nicene and Post-Nicene Fathers,* First Series, Vol. 13, ed. Philip Schaff, (New York: Cosimo Classics, 2007), 23.

died, you would say, "What an idiot!" But if one of your children was still in the house, and I said, "Let me show you how much I love you!" and ran into the fiery house and saved your child but died myself, you would say, "Behold, how he loved us!" Now if you can save yourself by works, Jesus' death is not loving; it is pure stupidity. If, however, you are lost and dying and unable to save yourself, his death means everything.[46]

Application

- How should this affect your view of the Christian life? We live by faith in the loving and self-giving Son of God. This is glorious, but it is not the same as living by sight. We live between the times, in the overlap of the ages. We live by faith but still have to fight the flesh, as will become clear in Galatians chapter five.
- Put off the old self (2:19-20). It is very interesting to see Paul's logic in the parallel passage of Romans 6. In verse 11, he commands us to consider ourselves dead to sin and alive to God. But previously in verse 2, he wrote that we are, in fact, dead to sin. Count yourself dead to sin because you are dead to sin. Let's appropriate these realities in everyday life. We no longer live. Christ lives in us. The life we do live is by faith in the Son of God.

Theological Defense: 3:1-4:11

The Experience of the Spirit (3:1-5)

Now we turn to the section of the letter where Paul begins his theological defense.

---

[46] Recounted in Keller, *Galatians,* 51-52.

1-2 *O foolish Galatians! Who has bewitched you? It was before your eyes that Jesus Christ was publicly portrayed as crucified. Let me ask you only this: Did you receive the Spirit by works of the law or by hearing with faith?*

Paul now turns to directly address the Galatians. The Galatians were being foolish. They were bewitched—a word used of being cast in a spell using black magic. Paul equates those who would force the old covenant on Christians with evil magicians. Satan is ultimately behind it all though. He always is. They were putting way too much stock in human ability, thinking we actually had the ability to gain God's favor by obeying the law. They were foolishly acting as if Christ had not been crucified, but in Paul's preaching, they had "seen" Christ crucified publicly. Notice the message that was preached: Jesus Christ crucified--the heart of the gospel. They were also foolishly forgetting what time it was in redemptive history. Paul has to remind them how they received the end-time gift of the Spirit. The end-time Spirit was promised in several places in the Hebrew Scriptures:

Isaiah 32:14-16 *For the palace is forsaken, the populous city deserted; the hill and the watchtower will become dens forever, a joy of wild donkeys, a pasture of flocks; until the Spirit is poured upon us from on high, and the wilderness becomes a fruitful field, and the fruitful field is deemed a forest. Then justice will dwell in the wilderness, and righteousness abide in the fruitful field.*

Isaiah 44:3 *For I will pour water on the thirsty land, and streams on the dry ground; I will pour my Spirit upon your offspring, and my blessing on your descendants.*

Ezekiel 36:25-27 *I will sprinkle clean water on you, and you shall be clean from all your uncleannesses, and from all your idols I will cleanse you. And I will give you a new heart, and a new spirit I will put within you. And I will remove the heart of stone from your flesh and give you a heart of flesh. And I will put my Spirit within you, and cause you to walk in my statutes and be careful to obey my rules.*

Joel 2:27-29 *You shall know that I am in the midst of Israel, and that I am the LORD your God and there is none else. And my people shall never again be put to shame. And it shall come to pass afterward, that I will pour out my Spirit on all flesh; your sons and your daughters shall prophesy, your old men shall dream dreams, and your young men shall see visions. Even on the male and female servants in those days I will pour out my Spirit.*

These promises came to fulfillment at Pentecost (Acts 2) and the Galatians had received the end-time gift of the Spirit through faith. This is decisive evidence that they had been justified by faith. The Spirit is the sign that one belongs to the people of God (1 Cor 2:12, Rom 5:5, 8:9). The new age is here. John Barclay writes, "In line with this eschatology, and in common with other early Christians, Paul interpreted the experience of the Spirit as the fulfillment of the promise (3:14) and the inauguration of 'the fullness of time' (Gal 4:4-6; cf. Rom 8:23; Acts 2:15-21)."[47] It is foolish to return to the old age.

3-5 *Are you so foolish? Having begun by the Spirit, are you now being perfected by the flesh? Did you suffer so many things in vain—if indeed it was in vain? Does he who supplies the Spirit to you and works miracles among you do so by works of the law, or by hearing with faith—*

Here, the flesh is our old person—who wewere in Adam. The NIV rightly interprets "flesh" in this context as "human effort." It is yet another contrast between this age

---

[47] Barclay, *Obeying the Truth*, 84.

and the age to come. Are you relying on the person you were in Adam, or the new person you are in Christ by the Spirit? The Galatians were beginning to do the former. We must do the latter.

Application

- Is your Christian life experiential? Some Christians over-emphasize their experience, but our tradition is often guilty of under-emphasizing experience. It is interesting that Paul here appeals to their experience of receiving the Spirit. We must be people of the Word and people of the Spirit. We must be intellectual *and* emotional Christians.
- Has your life changed since you have been converted? Faith isn't just an intellectual assent but an embracing of Jesus as Lord. As we will see in Galatians 5:6, faith works through love. To confess faith in Jesus is to bow to his Lordship over all aspects of your life.[48] What areas are you trying to hold onto?
- All of life is by faith. It is not the case that a person is justified by faith and then grows in holiness by human effort (3:3). Many think we simply believe the

---

[48] I was recently listening to a sermon by a guy advocating what has come to be known as "easy believism" or "cheap grace." He was appealing to the narrative about the Philippian jailer. He was saying that the apostles did not tell him to repent but only to *believe.* The problem with his position is that the apostles say, "Believe in the Lord Jesus Christ" (Acts 16:31). The title "Lord" has life-shattering implications. How often do we confess Jesus as "Lord" without realizing the weightiness of his lordship?

gospel to be justified, and are then sanctified by applying biblical principles. This approach misses the mark. Rather, we apply the gospel. In the moment of sin, we should ask ourselves, "What do I need at this moment?" A spouse without original sin? Self-parenting children? A throne we can sit on without interruption? What is being withheld that I feel I need in order to be complete? Whatever it is—it is playing the role of a functional savior. We think better kids, a holier wife, a more fulfilling job, or more promising circumstances will save us when only Jesus will do that. We don't need better circumstances. We need to grasp the glorious gospel of God. We are sanctified; we grow in holiness by applying the gospel to all of life, for it is the gospel that is the power of God for salvation (Rom 1:16).

Chapter 5
Galatians 3:6-14

Passage

...just as Abraham "believed God, and it was counted to him as righteousness"? Know then that it is those of faith who are the sons of Abraham. And the Scripture, foreseeing that God would justify the Gentiles by faith, preached the gospel beforehand to Abraham, saying, "In you shall all the nations be blessed." So then, those who are of faith are blessed along with Abraham, the man of faith. For all who rely on works of the law are under a curse; for it is written, "Cursed be everyone who does not abide by all things written in the Book of the Law, and do them." Now it is evident that no one is justified before God by the law, for "The righteous shall live by faith." But the law is not of faith, rather "The one who does them shall live by them." Christ redeemed us from the curse of the law by becoming a curse for us—for it is written, "Cursed is everyone who is hanged on a tree"—so that in Christ Jesus the blessing of Abraham might come to the Gentiles, so that we might receive the promised Spirit through faith.

The Benefits of Faith

6-7 *just as Abraham "believed God, and it was counted to him as righteousness"? Know then that it is those of faith who are the sons of Abraham.*

The Judaizers were appealing to Abraham as a model law-keeper. This is the emphasis found in Jewish inter-testamental literature as well,[49] but Paul wants to empha-

---

[49] John Barclay writes, "On the basis of Gen 26:5 ('Abraham obeyed my voice and kept my charge, my commandments, my statutes and my laws') and similar verses concerning

size his faith, not his obedience.[50] There is one way of salvation in both Testaments. Abraham believed God, and it was counted to him as righteousness. In the Genesis narrative, we find two very clear instances that show it is not his performance but God's provision that makes him righteous: his son's miraculous birth and God passing through the animals in the covenant ceremony while Abraham was asleep.

Galatians 3:7 is an inference from verse 6. Since Abraham was counted righteous because of his faith, know then that his true children are those of faith. This passage has significant implications for how we relate the church to Israel. In fact, this passage is the nail in the coffin for the system of theology known as Dispensationalism,which wants to make a tight distinction between the church and Israel. As we will see again and again in this letter, such a sharp distinction is not exegetically informed. Consider a couple of other clear passages in this regard:

> Galatians 3:29 *And if you are Christ's, then you are Abraham's offspring, heirs according to promise.*

> Romans 2:28-29 *For no one is a Jew who is merely one outwardly, nor is circumcision outward and physical. But a Jew is one inwardly, and circumcision is a matter of the heart, by the Spirit, not by the letter. His praise is not from man but from God.*

Abraham's obedience, it was assumed in Jewish traditions of many kinds that Abraham had kept the law even before its promulgation on Sinai," *Obeying the Truth,* 66.

[50] Ibid., 87.

Philippians 3:3 *For we are the real circumcision, who worship by the Spirit of God and glory in Christ Jesus and put no confidence in the flesh—*

We will see this truth expounded again and again in this letter. One of the main themes of the letter is that there is no such distinction.

8-9 *And the Scripture, foreseeing that God would justify the Gentiles by faith, preached the gospel beforehand to Abraham, saying, "In you shall all the nations be blessed." So then, those who are of faith are blessed along with Abraham, the man of faith.*

This is a fascinating passage. The main point is similar to the previous verse: it is those of faith who are blessed with Abraham. But Paul undergirds his reasoning by pointing out that the gospel was preached to Abraham when God made a covenant with him. The promises made in that covenant are coming to fulfillment now. The new age of fulfillment has arrived with the resurrection of Jesus.

God had promised Abraham a world-wide family. Through Jesus Christ, these promises were coming to fruition. Elsewhere, Paul writes:

"For I tell you that Christ became a servant to the circumcised to show God's truthfulness, in order to confirm the promises given to the patriarchs, and in order that the Gentiles might glorify God for his mercy. As it is written, "Therefore I will praise you among the Gentiles, and sing to your name." And again it is said, "Rejoice, O Gentiles, with his people." And again, "Praise the Lord, all you Gentiles, and let all the peoples extol him." And again Isaiah says, "The root of Jesse will come, even he who arises to rule the Gentiles; in him will the Gentiles hope." (Rom 15:8-12)

In this passage from Romans, Paul quotes from 2 Samuel 22:50, Psalm 18:49, Deuteronomy 32:43, Psalm 117:1, and Isaiah 11:10. The Creator's plan was always to include the

Gentiles. I will unpack this Old Testament theme more when we come to Galatians 6:16.

It is also very interesting that Paul personifies Scripture here. It is *Scripture* that foresaw and *Scripture* that preached. From this we can firmly agree with B.B. Warfield who famously noted, "What Scripture says, God says."

As mentioned above, many today want to emphasize the corporate aspects of Scripture to the neglect of the individual aspects. They love to point to the corporate promises like Genesis 12-18: all nations will be blessed through Abraham. This is great, but also note that Paul equates the gospel here with justification by faith. The word *foreseeing* is a participle modifying the verb "preach the gospel beforehand." The ESV does a good job with the commas in their translation. Scripture, foreseeing justification, preached the gospel beforehand. The gospel is not limited to justification, but certainly includes it.

The Dire Consequence of Not Having Faith

> 10 *For all who rely on works of the law are under a curse; for it is written, "Cursed be everyone who does not abide by all things written in the Book of the Law, and do them."*

In contrast to "those of faith" (Gal 3:7), "those of the works of the law"[51] are under a curse. You are under a curse because God says so (quoting Deut 27:26). What Scripture says, God says. The Judaizers were appealing to the Old Testament to bolster their case, and Paul is showing their erroneous interpretation. The very Scriptures they

[51] My translation. The ESV adds "rely on" to this verse, but this misses the contrast with "those of faith."

were appealing to show that what they are seeking to do will lead to a curse.[52] It is written:

> 11 *Now it is evident that no one is justified before God by the law, for "The righteous shall live by faith."*

It is evident, it's clear that no one is justified before God by the law. It is evident because no one does or abides by all things written in the book of the law. We disobey. It is also evident because that is not the way God works. Paul quotes Habakkuk 2:4 to show that the righteous shall live by faith. Notice how justification and life are parallel in this passage. There are some within the so-called "New Perspective on Paul" who are seeking to re-define justification to mean "included within the covenant people" instead of "being declared in the right." This passage (along with many others) flies in the face of that interpretation. Here, to be justified is to have life. "Life" here is eschatological life, the life of the age to come. Faith is the means to be justified and the means to eternal life.

> 12 *But the law is not of faith, rather "The one who does them shall live by them."*

It is also evident that no one is justified before God by the law because the law is not of faith. The law does not call on people to trust in the obedience of another, but to *do,* to *obey* its stipulations. The law doesn't give, but demands. Law and faith are mutually exclusive as bases for righteousness.

The law cannot provide the promised blessing because sinful humanity cannot obey it.

---

[52] As we will see in Galatians 6:13, the Judaizers themselves do not keep the law.

Paul is quoting Leviticus 18:5 here. Israel already enjoyed a covenantal relationship with the Lord in the context of this verse, but Paul cites this verse with a view to its conditional nature. To remain in the promised land was contingent on personal obedience to the law. They were called to obey, not to trust in another. This was not grace, according to the apostle Paul. Paul sees three problems with the law-covenant: First, there is the *human* problem—we can't obey it. Next, he pinpoints the problem with the *nature* of the law—it cannot provide salvation. Last, he points out the *oldness* of the old covenant—it is part of the old age, not the new age, which is characterized by the power of the Holy Spirit.[53]

Because the old covenant has been abrogated, the gracious provision via the sacrificial system is no longer in place. So to turn to the law-covenant now requires perfect obedience, which clearly no one does. This is why Paul can say that if anyone accepts even circumcision, he is obligated to keep the whole law (Gal 5:3). To turn to the old covenant, after Jesus has come, is to be severed from Christ, fallen away from grace (Gal 5:4).

Christ's Gracious Intervention

> 13 *Christ redeemed us from the curse of the law by becoming a curse for us—for it is written, "Cursed is everyone who is hanged on a tree"—*

Thanks be to God for his indescribable gift! We were under a curse,but Christ has redeemed us. How did he do it? By becoming a curse for us—Oh sweet exchange. Christ

---

[53] Jason Meyer, *The End of the Law* (Nashville: B&H Academic, 2009), 140-163.

was our substitute. He took the penalty we deserved. For our sakes God made him to be sin who knew no sin, so that in him we might become the righteousness of God (2 Cor 5:21).

God had "redeemed" Israel from their slavery to Egypt. We, Gentiles, were not under Egyptian bondage, but were in bondage to sin, cursed by the law. Christ has come and brought about the new exodus with his death and resurrection and bought us back. Through faith, we have been redeemed.

The Results of Christ's Gracious and Glorious Intervention

> 14 *so that in Christ Jesus the blessing of Abraham might come to the Gentiles, so that we might receive the promised Spirit through faith.*

Here, the Holy Spirit through Paul gives us two results (*hina*) of Christ's redeeming death for those who believe: the Gentiles receive the blessing of Abraham and the Holy Spirit. In this verse, "Gentiles" is front-loaded for emphasis: *to the Gentiles the blessing of Abraham will come in Christ Jesus*! By mentioning both Spirit and blessing, Paul probably has Isaiah 44:3 in mind in this verse, which reads, *"For I will pour water on the thirsty land, and streams on the dry ground; I will pour my* Spirit *upon your offspring, and my* blessing *on your descendants."*

For Paul, receiving the Holy Spirit is the fulfillment of the promises given to Abraham. The age of fulfillment is *now*. God is blessing Jews and Gentiles who trust in Christ with the promised Holy Spirit. Abraham's family is growing.

This is indeed a beautiful and theologically rich passage. In our day, it is popular to be a "person of faith." We often hear people say, "Just have faith." But without objective content, "faith" is just positive thinking with no objective foundation. This is an Oprah gospel, which is no gospel. I want to point out six reasons from this section why you should have faith *in Christ,* not just have an ambiguous faith:

1. Because you will become a child of Abraham

   3:7 *Know then that it is those of faith who are the sons of Abraham.*

2. Because unbelief results in being cursed

   3:10 *For all who rely on works of the law are under a curse; for it is written, "Cursed be everyone who does not abide by all things written in the Book of the Law, and do them."*

3. Because by faith, you will live

   3:11 *Now it is evident that no one is justified before God by the law, for "The righteous shall live by faith."*

4. Because we obtain redemption

   3:13 *Christ redeemed us from the curse of the law by becoming a curse for us—for it is written, "Cursed is everyone who is hanged on a tree"—*

5. Because we are blessed with Abraham

   3:9 *So then, those who are of faith are blessed along with Abraham, the man of faith.*

   3:14 *so that in Christ Jesus the blessing of Abraham might come to the Gentiles*

6. Because we will receive the promised Holy Spirit

   3:14 *so that we might receive the promised Spirit through faith.*

Application

- Trust Christ for your right standing, not yourself. Our tendency is to try to be our own savior by our own performance. Trying to earn favor with God will inevitably result in one of two errors: self-love or self-hate. Either we will think we are keeping our end of the deal and think too highly of ourselves as a result; or we will (more realistically) realize we are not keeping our end of the deal and live in constant discouragement. Satan pushes us to derive our worth from what we can do. Do we parent well? Are we athletic? Do we have a good job? Are we as attractive as the people on the magazine covers? But we must realize that we contribute nothing. We are declared in the right by faith *alone*. We must learn this every day, because we are prone to wander. Martin Luther writes, "Particularly when you hear an immature and unripe saint trumpet that he knows very well that we must be saved by the grace of God, without our own works, and then pretend that this is a snap for him, well, then we have no doubt that he has no idea of what he is talking about and probably will never find out. For this is not an art that can be completely learned or of which anyone could boast that he is a master. It is an art that will always have us as pupils while it remains the master. And all those who do understand and practice it do not boast that they can do everything. On the contrary, they sense it like a wonderful taste or odor that they greatly desire and pursue; and they are amazed that they cannot grasp it or comprehend it as they would like. They hunger, thirst, and yearn for it more and more; and they never tire of hearing about or dealing with it, just as St. Paul himself confessed that he has not yet obtained it (Phil. 3:12). And in Matt. 5:6 Christ calls those blessed who hunger and thirst after righteousness."[54]

- Church Historian Richard Lovelace writes, "Only a fraction of the present body of professing Christians are solidly appropriating the justifying work of Christ in their lives. Many have so light an apprehension of God's holiness and of the extent and guilt of their sin that consciously they see little need for justification, although below the surface of their lives they are deeply guilt-ridden and insecure. Many others have a theoretical commitment to this doctrine, but in their day-to-day existence they rely on their sanctification for their justification … drawing their assurance of acceptance with God from their sincerity, their past experience of conversion, their recent religious performance or the relative infrequency of their conscious, willful disobedience. Few know enough to start each day with a thoroughgoing stand upon Luther's platform: *you are accepted,* looking outward in faith and claiming the wholly alien righteousness of Christ as the only ground for acceptance, relaxing in that quality of

---

[54] Martin Luther, "Psalm 117," trans. Edward Sittler in *Selected Psalms III* from *Luther's Works,* vol. 14, ed Jaroslav Pelikan (St. Louis: Concordia, 1958), 37 quoted in Schreiner, *Galatians,* 139.

trust which will produce increasing sanctification as faith is active in love and gratitude."

- Give thanks to God for keeping his promise to Abraham and showing mercy to the Gentiles. I, for one, would not be writing this if it were not for God's promise to those were formerly separated from the Messiah, alienated from the commonwealth of Israel, and strangers to the covenants of promise, having no hope and without God in the world (Eph 2:12). What a gracious God this is.
- Another implication from God keeping his promises to Abraham is that we live in the "era of witness." We have the privilege and responsibility of helping God fulfill his promise by proclaiming the good news to the nations. The descendants of Abraham will be as numerous as the stars. Abraham is still counting and it is the mission of the church to bear witness to the risen Christ and so increase Abraham's family.
- Do you live in constant guilt? After all, you could pray more, give more, be more bold in evangelism, watch less TV, downsize the house, go to one vehicle, recycle more, and on and on. But is this God's will for your life? No, we are meant to live in freedom (as we will see in Ch. 5), and joy in the Holy Spirit. When Satan, the ultimate enemy and accuser, shoots his fiery darts your way—remind him of your standing with God through Christ. I am reminded of a beautiful song by Shane and Shane:

"The father of lies
Coming to steal
Kill and destroy
All my hopes of being good enough
I hear him saying cursed are the ones
Who can't abide
He's right
Halleluia he's right!

The devil is preaching
The song of the redeemed
That I am cursed and gone astray
I cannot gain salvation
Embracing accusation

Could the father of lies
Be telling the truth
Of God to me tonight?
If the penalty of sin is death
Then death is mine
I hear him saying cursed are the ones
Who can't abide
He's right
Alleluia he's right!

Oh the devil's singing over me
An age old song
That I am cursed and gone astray
Singing the first verse so conveniently
He's forgotten the refrain
Jesus saves!"[55]

When you grasp the glorious good news that Jesus—not you or anything else—saves, you are transformed and live lives that reflect the gospel.

---

[55] Shane and Shane, "Embracing Accusation."

Chapter 6: Galatians 3:15-25

Passage

To give a human example, brothers: even with a man-made covenant, no one annuls it or adds to it once it has been ratified. Now the promises were made to Abraham and to his offspring. It does not say, "And to offsprings," referring to many, but referring to one, "And to your offspring," who is Christ. This is what I mean: the law, which came 430 years afterward, does not annul a covenant previously ratified by God, so as to make the promise void. For if the inheritance comes by the law, it no longer comes by promise; but God gave it to Abraham by a promise. Why then the law? It was added because of transgressions, until the offspring should come to whom the promise had been made, and it was put in place through angels by an intermediary. Now an intermediary implies more than one, but God is one. Is the law then contrary to the promises of God? Certainly not! For if a law had been given that could give life, then righteousness would indeed be by the law. But the Scripture imprisoned everything under sin, so that the promise by faith in Jesus Christ might be given to those who believe. Now before faith came, we were held captive under the law, imprisoned until the coming faith would be revealed. So then, the law was our guardian until Christ came, in order that we might be justified by faith. But now that faith has come, we are no longer under a guardian,

We continue to unpack Paul's theological defense (Gal 3-4:11). This section is theologically weighty. Here we come to the heart of the differences between Paul and his opponents. We also gain a *Christian* understanding of the old covenant law.

Salvation History: The Abrahamic Covenant takes precedence over the temporary Mosaic Covenant (3:15-18)

> 15 *To give a human example, brothers: even with a man-made covenant, no one annuls it or adds to it once it has been ratified.*

Again, Paul calls the Galatians *brothers*. He is calling his brothers and sisters in Christ back to the gospel with the gospel. Paul uses an example from everyday life to show that people don't set a covenant aside or add to it. Even among human beings, people don't add to or annul covenants once they have been ratified. If this is true in human affairs, how much more with God!

> 16 *Now the promises were made to Abraham and to his offspring. It does not say, "And to offsprings," referring to many, but referring to one, "And to your offspring," who is Christ.*

"Seed" is a collective noun, only used in the singular in the Old Testament. Genesis 22:17 says, "I will surely bless you, and I will surely multiply your offspring as the stars of heaven and as the sand that is on the seashore. And *your offspring* shall possess the gate of his enemies." The pronoun here is singular. Genesis holds out the promise that a seed will come to crush the head of the enemy. This promise first occurs in the "first gospel announcement" in Genesis 3:15: "I will put enmity between you and the woman, and between your offspring and her offspring; he shall bruise your head, and you shall bruise his heel." Continuing the storyline, God promises to bless Abraham and his seed, and says that he will have kings as descendants (17:6). Judah is told that the scepter would not depart from his family line, and then David is promised that his seed will have an everlasting throne. Jesus arrives on the scene as "the son of David, the son of Abraham" (Matt 1:1). Christ is the true seed of Abraham. He is the one who receives the promises. All of God's promises find their yes *in him*. He is the one and only heir (last Adam, faithful David, true Israel), and therefore his people share his inheritance. Jesus is the representative offspring of Abraham and David and is the ultimate fulfillment of Genesis 3:15. Christ is the hermeneutical key that unlocks all of Scripture.

> 17 *This is what I mean: the law, which came 430 years afterward, does not annul a covenant previously ratified by God, so as to make the promise void.*

Paul is reading the Bible as a story. He is showing that God's plan has historical sequence: Abraham—Law—Messiah. The law came 430 years after the promise to Abraham.[56] This is not what most Jewish people believed. For example, Sirach 44:19-20 says, "Abraham was the great father of a multitude of nations, and no one has been found like him in glory. He kept the law of the Most High, and entered into a covenant with him."[57] The Jewish people were not correctly reading the Bible as God has given it. They were not reading with a beginning, middle, and an end. The Law had a definite starting point and a definite ending point. It was to be in effect *after* the promise *until* the Messiah. This is very clear from this chapter. The promise was given before the law, and the addition of the law does not annul the promise. Paul is showing them how to read their Bible.

---

[56] N.T. Wright notes that this chapter is "soaked in Abraham, and every section depends on the sense of a *historical sequence* in which Abraham comes first, the law comes next, and the Messiah—and/or 'faith'—comes to complete the sequence," *Justification*, 123.

[57] Quoted in Meyer, *The End of the Law*, 171.

I mentioned above that when Paul says "law" (*nomos),* he is referring to the Mosaic covenant. The law is bound up with the covenant. We see this very clearly in Exodus. It is important to read the Bible as it is presented to us, on its own terms. As tempting as it may be at times, theological constructs must not be imposed on the text. There are many people who seek to divide the law up into three categories: civil, ceremonial, and moral. This was really systematized by Thomas Aquinas in the thirteenth century. The problem with this three-fold division is the Bible. The literary structure of this covenant is very important for seeing that the old covenant is a package deal, a unit.[58] The law cannot be extrapolated from the covenant. Exodus chapters 19 and 24 frame the "book of the covenant": chapters 20-23. Chapter 19 is the background and chapter 24 describes the ceremony of covenant ratification. Exodus 20:1 introduces the 10 words and Exodus 21:1 introduces the rules of 21-23. The rules of chapters 21-23 are applications of the 10 words of chapter 20 to specific social situations. Chapters 20 and 21-23 constitute specific sections of the covenant that cannot be separated. You can't take the words as eternal and the rules as temporary because both sections together constitute the book of the covenant. This is how the text is given to us. Exodus 24:3 bears this out:

---

[58] See Peter Gentry, "The Covenant at Sinai," SBJT 12.3, Fall 08, 38-63. On this point (and many others), the Anabaptists had it right. See "Anabaptists and the New Covenant," by David M. Moffitt, http://www.kindredminds.org/Articles/anabaptists_nc.html. Accessed July 7, 2007.

"Moses came and told the people *all the words* of the LORD and *all the rules*. And all the people answered with one voice and said, 'All the words that the LORD has spoken we will do'" (italics mine). Notice that it says the words (ch. 20) and the rules (ch. 21-23). In Exodus 24:7, Moses calls this the "book of the covenant." Seeing the connections here shows the impossibility of new covenant Christians being under this law. Consider the following sarcastic letter:

> Thank you for doing so much to educate people regarding God's law. I have learned a great deal from you, and try to share that knowledge with as many people as I can. When someone tries to defend the homosexual lifestyle, for example, I simply remind them that Leviticus 18:22 clearly states it to be an abomination—end of debate. I do need some advice from you, however, regarding some other elements of God's laws and how to follow them.
>
> 1. Leviticus 25:44 states that I may possess slaves, both male and female, provided they are purchased from neighboring nations. A friend of mine claims that this applies to Mexicans but not Canadians. Can you clarify? Why can't I own Canadians?
>
> 2. I would like to sell my daughter into slavery, as sanctioned in Exodus 21:7. In this day and age, what do you think would be a fair price for her?
>
> 3. I know that I am allowed no contact with a woman while she is in her period of menstrual uncleanliness (Lev 15:19-24). The problem is: how do I tell? I have tried asking, but most women take offense.
>
> 4. When I burn a bull on the altar as a sacrifice, I know it creates a pleasing odor to the Lord (Lev 1:9). The problem is my neighbors. They claim the odor is not pleasing to them. Should I smite them?

5. I have a neighbor who insists on working on the Sabbath. Exodus 35:2 clearly states he should be put to death. Am I morally obligated to kill him myself, or should I ask the police to do it?

6. A friend of mine feels that even though eating shellfish is an abomination (Lev 11:10), it is a lesser abomination than homosexuality. I don't agree. Can you settle this? Are there degrees of abomination?

7. Leviticus 21:20 states that I may not approach the altar of God if I have a defect in my sight. I have to admit that I wear reading glasses. Does my vision have to be 20/20, or is there some wiggle room there?

8. Most of my male friends get their hair trimmed, including the hair around their temples, even though this is expressly forbidden by Leviticus 19:27. How should they die?

9. I know from Leviticus 11:6-8 that touching the skin of a dead pig makes me unclean, but may I still play football if I wear gloves?

10. My uncle has a farm. He violates Leviticus 19:19 by planting two different crops in the same field, as does his wife by wearing garments made of two different kinds of thread (cotton-polyester blend). He also tends to curse and blaspheme a lot. Is it really necessary that we go to all the trouble of getting the whole town together to stone them (Lev 24:10-16)? Couldn't we just burn them to death at a private family affair, like we do with people who sleep with their in-laws (Lev 20:14)?

I know you have studied these things extensively and thus enjoy considerable expertise in such matters, so I am con-

> fident you can help. Thank you again for reminding us that God's word is eternal and unchanging.[59]

The law constitutes the stipulations of the covenant.[60] To break the law is to break the covenant (see Deut 17:2, 2 Kin 17:15, 18:12, Hos 8:1).

> 18 *For if the inheritance comes by the law, it no longer comes by promise; but God gave it to Abraham by a promise.*

The inheritance (which, as we have seen, includes a right standing, the Holy Spirit, and ultimately the whole world) comes by promise, not by law. Here we see that the Abrahamic covenant and the Sinai covenant are of a different *nature*. One is characterized by law and the other is characterized by promise. They operate on different planes and principles. When it comes to our standing before God, they are mutually exclusive.

John Murray is one of the most famous covenant theologians in recent history.[61] His neglect of the biblical text is astounding to me in this regard. He writes that we are giv-

---

[59] Garry Wills, *What Jesus Meant* (New York: Penguin, 2006), 34-35 quoted in Shane Claiborne and Chris Haw, *Jesus for President* (Grand Rapids: Zondervan, 2008), 50-51. For the impossibility of Christians following the law, also see David Dorsey's excellent article, "The Law of Moses and the Christian: A Compromise." *JETS* 34.3 (September 1991): 321-34.

[60] Contra T.D. Alexander who says there are two documents with two sets of obligations in *From Paradise to the Promised Land* (Grand Rapids: Baker, 2002), 176-77.

[61] It should be noted that Murray admits that his version of Covenant Theology is a recasting of traditional Covenant Theology.

en no reason "for construing the Mosaic covenant in terms different from those of the Abrahamic. ... What needs to be emphasized now is that the Mosaic covenant in respect of the condition of obedience is not in a different category from the Abrahamic. It is too frequently assumed that the conditions prescribed in connection with the Mosaic covenant place the Mosaic dispensation in a demand or obligation, on the other. In reality there is nothing that is principally different in the necessity of keeping the covenant and of obedience to God's voice, which proceeds from the Mosaic covenant, from that which is involved in the keeping required in the Abrahamic"[62] One wonders if Murray ever wrestled with Galatians chapter three?

T. David Gordon, professor of Greek and Religion at Grove City College, in an essay on Galatians 3:6-14, says that Murray overreacted to Dispensationalism.[63] Hence, he sought to disprove their system by (over) emphasizing the continuity between the two Testaments. Gordon observes that he also had a tendency to seek systematic coherence at the expense of exegesis. To Gordon's knowledge, from 1931-73, out of 221 reviews, articles, essays, and books, there is not so much as a paragraph about Galatians! Galatians 3-4 is the first place I am going when it comes to the issue of continuity/discontinuity. The problem with John

[62] John Murray, *The Covenant of Grace* (Phillipsburg, NJ: P&R Publishing, 1953), 20, 22.

[63] T. David Gordon, "Abraham and Sinai Contrasted in Galatians 3:6-14," in *The Law is Not of Faith: Essays on Works and Grace in the Mosaic Covenant* (Phillipsburg, NJ: P&R Publishing, 2009), 240-58.

Murray's brand of Covenant Theology is that it is not exegetically grounded. It is admirable to seek to show the coherence of God's Word, but we don't want to seek continuity where God has revealed discontinuity.

In this same essay, Gordon helpfully outlines five contrasts between the Abrahamic covenant and the Mosaic covenant:

> 1. The Abrahamic Covenant Includes the Gentiles while the Old Covenant Excludes Them.
>
> 2. The Abrahamic Covenant Blesses While the Sinai Covenant Curses
>
> 3. The Abrahamic Covenant is Characterized by Faith while the Sinai Covenant is characterized by Works of the Law
>
> 4. The Abrahamic Covenant Justifies while the Sinai Covenant Does Not
>
> 5. The Abrahamic Covenant is Referred to as "Promise" while the Sinai Covenant is Referred to as "Law."[64]

Purpose of the Law: The Christian understanding of the Mosaic Law (3:19-25)

> 19-20 *Why then the law? It was added because of transgressions, until the offspring should come to whom the promise had been made, and it was put in place through angels by an intermediary. Now an intermediary implies more than one, but God is one.*

This passage should be primary when it comes to our understanding of the law. Paul says the law was added "because of transgressions" (*parabaseōn charin*). This should be interpreted as "to increase transgression." This is clear in the history of Israel. The giving of the law did not result

---

[64] Ibid., 243-50.

in a God-centered, law-abiding society, but rather, it produced exile. So Stephen Dempster writes, "Sinai does something profoundly negative to Israel."[65] He illustrates: Murmuring before the giving of the law was not judged (Exod 17:2-7), but is judged severely after the law (Num 11:1-3). Also, pre-law Sabbath violations bring a reprimand (Exod 16:27-30), while post-law Sabbath violations bring death (Num 15:32-36). Before the law, Israel succeeds against the Amalekites (Exod 17:8-16) but they fail miserably after the law (Num 14:41-44).

Galatians 3:22 also says that "the Scripture imprisoned everything under sin." This same truth is clearly taught in Romans 5:20: "Now the law came in to increase the trespass, but where sin increased, grace abounded all the more." It is evident that John Bunyan believed the same thing from his writing in *The Pilgrim's Progress.*[66] There he writes of a parlor full of dust. A man comes in with a broom to begin sweeping the floor, but it just shifts the dust around, clouding the room and choking Christian. Then a damsel brings water to sprinkle the floor, which made it sweep clean. The parlor is the depraved heart; the broom is the law; the dust is original sin; the water is the gospel of grace. Applying the law to the unredeemed heart simply stirs up the dust; it does not clean the filthy heart.

Paul's view of the law was clearly at odds with the common Jewish understanding. Jewish people believed

---

[65] Stephen Dempster, *Dominion and Dynasty* (Downers Grove, IL: 20), 112-13.

[66] John Bunyan, *The Pilgrim's Progress* (Grand Rapids: Spire), 21-22.

that the law led to life. They also believed in the eternality of the law. It was called imperishable, immortal, and changeless.[67] But Paul shows that it was *never meant* to be permanent. It was, by divine design, temporary. Notice the word *until,* which is clearly a temporal indicator. Paul uses this word here in verse 19, but also three other times in the immediate context:

> 3:23 *Now before faith came, we were held captive under the law, imprisoned until the coming faith would be revealed.*
>
> 3:24 *So then, the law was our guardian until Christ came, in order that we might be justified by faith.*
>
> 4:2 *but he is under guardians and managers until the date set by his father.*

Galatians 3:20 is notoriously obscure. Some have said there are 250-300 interpretations of the passage and one commentator draws on the 430 years to say there are 430 interpretations.[68] But, the presence of a mediator shows its inferiority. It excludes the possibility of a direct revelation by God. The law was delivered by Moses and angels, but God came directly to Abraham.

> 21 *Is the law then contrary to the promises of God? Certainly not! For if a law had been given that could give life, then righteousness would indeed be by the law.*

Since Paul has been set on showing the limitations of the law, one might expect the answer to this question to be yes. Rather, the answer is "Certainly not," "May it never be!" The law is not opposed to the promises. God has one plan, but the covenants have differing functions that work to-

---

[67] Longenecker, *Galatians,* 139.

[68] See Schreiner, *Galatians,* 207.

gether in a complementary way within that plan. The law was not able nor *designed* to secure righteousness, inheritance, or life. God did not design the law to give life. The law serves the promise in that it shows that the only way to gain a right standing is through Christ crucified. From Galatians 3, we see five problems with the law:

1. It curses
2. It is based on doing, not believing
3. Christ must intervene
4. The law is unable and not designed to secure righteousness, inheritance, or life
5. The law brings transgression[69]

Also note the assumption is that we need to be given life! This assumes that we are spiritually dead. We are not in need of heart surgery, but heart replacement.

Galatians 3:21b-25 is the answer to the question given in Galatians 3:21a: "Is the law opposed to the promises?"

> 22-23 *But the Scripture imprisoned everything under sin, so that the promise by faith in Jesus Christ might be given to those who believe. Now before faith came, we were held captive under the law, imprisoned until the coming faith would be revealed.*

One of the primary purposes of the law was to bring all humanity under the curse of the law. Here, Paul uses "faith" to refer to the new era of redemptive history, the time of fulfillment. It is an objective reality that demands a subjective response. Faith has come in redemptive history, and now demands faith in Jesus.

---

[69] Meyer, *The End of the Law,* 153, 161, 170.

In these verses, to be under law is to be under sin. The word *under* is important in this section as well. He uses it here in verses 22 (imprisoned everything *under* sin) and 23 (held captive *under* the law), as well as in seven other places in Galatians:

> 3:10 *For all who rely on works of the law are under a curse; for it is written, "Cursed be everyone who does not abide by all things written in the Book of the Law, and do them."*
>
> 3:25 *But now that faith has come, we are no longer under a guardian,*
>
> 4:2 *but he is under guardians and managers until the date set by his father.*
>
> 4:4 *But when the fullness of time had come, God sent forth his Son, born of woman, born under the law,*
>
> 4:5 *to redeem those who were under the law, so that we might receive adoption as sons.*
>
> 4:21 *Tell me, you who desire to be under the law, do you not listen to the law?*
>
> 5:18 *But if you are led by the Spirit, you are not under the law.*

Paul personifies Scripture again in this verse as well. It is the Scripture, which from the context means the law, that imprisons. What Scripture says, God says. What Scripture does, God does. He is the God who acts by speaking.[70]

> 24-25 *So then, the law was our guardian until Christ came, in order that we might be justified by faith. But now that faith has come, we are no longer under a guardian,*

The word that Paul uses for *guardian* (*paidagōgos)* is important in the structure of Paul's argument here. Paul was

---

[70] See Timothy Ward, *Words of Life* (Downers Grove, IL: IVP Academic, 2009).

not using the term in an educational sense, despite our use of the derivative "pedagogue." Richard N. Longenecker writes, "For while today we think of pedagogues as teachers, in antiquity a *paidagōgos* was distinguished from a *didaskalos* ('teacher') and had custodial and disciplinary functions rather than educative or instructional ones."[71] In ancient Greco-Roman society, the *paidagōgos* was a domestic slave within the household who was responsible for supervising the children from infancy to late adolescence.[72] The "guardian" was clearly distinguished from the "teacher" in the Greco-Roman world. To cite just one example, consider Plato's *Lysis*, which has this account:

> Do [your parents] let you control your own self, or will they not trust you in that either? Of course they do not, he replied. But someone controls you? Yes, he said, my [guardian] here. Is he a slave? Why certainly; he belongs to us, he said. What a strange thing, I exclaimed: a free man controlled by a slave! But how does this [guardian] exert his control over you? By taking me to the teacher [*eis didaskalon*], he replied.[73]

Paidagōgos is probably best translated *babysitter*[74] in this context, as Paul clearly uses the term to refer to the law-

---

[71] Longenecker, *Galatians*, 146.

[72] See Frank Thielman, *Paul and the Law* (Downers Grove, IL: IVP, 1994) 132; Longenecker, *Galatians*, 148.

[73] Plato, *Lysis*, 208c, quoted in Longenecker, *Galatians*, 146.

[74] Schreiner, *New Testament Theology* (Grand Rapids: Baker, 2008), 366, 534, 646; N.T. Wright summarizes well: "So, then, the Torah was our nanny, our babysitter, the slave hired to look after us while we were young and at risk, so that we might make it through to the coming of the Messiah, when God's

covenant's temporal nature.[75] Guardians were only needed until maturity was reached, then they became unnecessary. John Chrysostom writes,

> The Law then, as it was our tutor, and we were kept shut under it, is not the adversary but the fellow-worker of grace; but if when grace is come, it continues to hold us down, it becomes an adversary; for if it confines those who ought to go forward to grace, then it is the destruction of our salvation. If a candle which gave light by night, kept us, when it became day, from the sun, it would not only not benefit, it would injure us and so doth the Law, if it stands between us and greater benefits.[76]

The law also functioned to show the human inability of being justified by the law. As Luther says, "The principal point, therefore, of the law in true Christian theology is to make people not better but worse; that is to say, it shows them their sin, so that they may be humbled, terrified, bruised, and broken and by this means may be driven to seek comfort and so to come to that blessed Seed."[77] In other words,

> To run and work the law commands,
> Yet gives me neither feet nor hands;

---

people would be defined, justified, declared to be God's people indeed, on the basis of faith," *Justification,* 129.

[75] Douglas Moo, "The Law of Moses or the Law of Christ," in John S. Feinberg, ed., *Continuity and Discontinuity: Perspectives on the Relationship Between the Old and New Testaments* (Wheaton, IL: Crossway Books, 1988), 214.

[76] Chrysostom, *Commentary on Galatians*, 29.

[77] Luther, *Galatians,* 176.

But better news the gospel brings:
It bids me fly and gives me wings[78]

Application

- Always test theological systems by Scripture. We affirm *sola Scriptura.* Now, let's act on our affirmation. Scripture must inform our theology. The three-fold division of the law is not biblical. It is an imposition on the text by a theological agenda.
- While there is not a three-fold division in the law, there is a three-fold problem with the law: people can't keep it, it doesn't give what it commands, and it is part of the old age.[79]
- The Abrahamic covenant and the Mosaic covenant are different in *kind.* In Scripture, there is no such thing as a single covenant of grace that spans all the covenants. Again, exegesis must inform theology. If we take the text seriously, we see that there are multiple covenants, and each one must be examined in its own in context before it is harmonized with the rest of the biblical covenants. We cannot flatten out the Bible. Paul shows that there is a law/promise contrast. Paul also shows us that they are not opposed. There is one plan of God which includes a contrast between the covenants.

The Bible gives us history, and this history is important for interpretation (cf. Rom 4, Heb 7). Pay attention to where

---

[78] Quoted in Meyer, *The End of the Law,* 2.

[79] Ibid., 153, 161.

you are in God's story as you read the Bible. God is the author of history.

Chapter 7:
Galatians 3:26-4:7

Passage

For in Christ Jesus you are all sons of God, through faith. For as many of you as were baptized into Christ have put on Christ. There is neither Jew nor Greek, there is neither slave nor free, there is no male and female, for you are all one in Christ Jesus. And if you are Christ's, then you are Abraham's offspring, heirs according to promise. I mean that the heir, as long as he is a child, is no different from a slave, though he is the owner of everything, but he is under guardians and managers until the date set by his father. In the same way we also, when we were children, were enslaved to the elementary principles of the world. But when the fullness of time had come, God sent forth his Son, born of woman, born under the law, to redeem those who were under the law, so that we might receive adoption as sons. And because you are sons, God has sent the Spirit of his Son into our hearts, crying, "Abba! Father!" So you are no longer a slave, but a son, and if a son, then an heir through God.

Abraham's Offspring are not "under law" but "in Christ" (3:26-29)

Paul is continuing his theological defense. This section supports the point that we are no longer under the babysitter. We no longer live under the terms of the law. The Judaizers were saying that true children of Abraham must obey the law to be justified, but Paul is saying that we are Abraham's offspring through faith in the true seed of Abraham, Jesus Christ.

26 *for in Christ Jesus you are all sons of God, through faith.*

Through faith, we are all—Jew or Gentile—sons of God. The reason he doesn't say sons and daughters is not because Paul was opposed to women. He uses "sons" because in that context, it was the son who received the inheritance rights (usually the firstborn). So in this sense, all of us—male and female –are "sons" of God.

27 For as many of you as were baptized into Christ have put on Christ.

We are sons of God because we are united with THE Son of God. We were baptized into him. We were baptized into him when we were baptized with water. We died and were raised with Christ when he died, and we apply these redemptive benefits when we are baptized in our own life experience.

Sometimes people get uncomfortable with this sort of language. Am I saying that baptism is what unites us with Christ? No, Paul is. Romans 6:3 says, "Do you not know that all of us who have been baptized into Christ Jesus were baptized into his death? We were buried therefore with him by baptism into death, in order that, just as Christ was raised from the dead by the glory of the Father, we too might walk in newness of life." Now, before you dismiss me (or Paul!) as a false teacher, we need to understand what baptism means in the New Testament. Notice the parallel with Galatians 3:26 and 3:27. Verse 26 says "you are all" sons of God through faith, which is parallel to "For as many of you" as were baptized in verse 27.[80] To have

---

[80] Longenecker, *Galatians,* 155. Longenecker writes, "The close association of faith and baptism in Paul (and throughout the NT), however, must never blind us to the fact that these are two distinct features of the one complex of Christian initiation."

faith is to be baptized.[81] An unbaptized believer would have been unheard of to the New Testament writers. As Tom Schreiner writes, "Since unbaptized Christians were virtually nonexistent, to refer to those who were baptized is another way of describing those who are Christians, those who have put their faith in Christ."[82]

According to the New Testament, faith, baptism, repentance, confession of Jesus as Lord, and receiving the Spirit are all different yet integral parts of becoming a Christian.[83] Robert Stein uses getting married as a helpful analogy. Marriage has several components that are inter-related and belong together: the saying of vows, the giving and receiving of rings; the pronouncement of marriage by the pastor; the signing of the marriage license, and the sexual consummation. If a person were to ask when I was married, what would I say? All of these components are involved in becoming married. You wouldn't want to isolate any of the

---

[81] So Michael Gorman says, "What Paul says of baptism, therefore, he would say also of faith. For instance, according to Galatians 3:27, people are 'baptized into Christ,' but according to Galatians 2:16, people 'believed into Christ'," *Cruciformity,* 123-24.

[82] Thomas R. Scheiner, *Romans. BECNT* (Grand Rapids: Baker, 1998), 306.

[83] Robert Stein, "Baptism in Luke-Acts," 36 in *Believer's Baptistm,* ed. Thomas R. Schreiner and Shawn D. Wright (Nashville: B&H Academic, 2006). He writes, "In the experience of becoming a Christian, five integrally related components took place at the same time, usually on the same day: repentance, faith, confession, receiving the gift of the Holy Spirit, and baptism," 52.

components from one another.[84] So it is with faith, baptism, receiving the Spirit, repentance, and confessing Christ as Lord and Savior. As an aside, I cannot continue without mentioning the fact that these realities cannot be said of *infants.*

As we have seen, Paul emphasizes the necessity of faith throughout Galatians. As mentioned early on, it is important to note how Paul *does not* argue. He does not say that baptism simply replaces circumcision, the very thing we would expect him to do if he believed that. It would have made it really easy to put the Judaizers in their place. As Richard Longenecker writes, "Paul is not simply replacing one external rite (circumcision) by another external rite (baptism). If that were so (*i.e.*, if he viewed baptism as a supplement to faith in much the same way that the Judaizers viewed circumcision as a supplement to faith) he could have simply settled the dispute at Galatia by saying that Christian baptism now replaces Jewish circumcision. He would certainly have saved himself a great deal of argument. But Paul saw baptism in no such light. Rather, while faith and baptism are part and parcel of becoming a Christian, they are always to be distinguished. Each has its own function, with baptism never to be viewed as having *ex opera operato* efficacy or as being a supplement to faith."[85]

The text says that we have put on Christ. To put on Christ means to take on his characteristics and virtues. To put on Christ is to become like him. Elsewhere Paul speaks

---

[84] Ibid., 57-58.

[85] Longenecker, *Galatians,* 156.

of putting on the new self, which is the same idea.[86] We put off the old person: who we are in Adam, and put on the new self: who we are in Christ. In other words, it is no longer I who live, but Christ who lives in me (Gal 2:20).

28 *There is neither Jew nor Greek, there is neither slave nor free, there is no male and female, for you are all one in Christ Jesus.*

In Christ, we are all one. This was, and is, very counter-cultural. For example, the beginning of the Jewish cycle of morning prayer said, "Blessed be He [God] that He did not make me a Gentile; blessed be He that He did not make me a boor [*i.e.*, an ignorant peasant or slave]; blessed be He that He did not make me a woman."[87] Similar expressions of gratitude appear in Greek writings as well. For example, "that I was born a human being and not a beast, next, a man and not a woman, thirdly, a Greek and not a barbarian."[88] Paul is showing us that the coming of Christ has flipped these sorts of divisions on their head. Douglas Moo writes, "Those who belong to Christ constitute a 'new humanity,' within which the distinctions of this world, while not obliterated, are relativized."[89] Colossians 3:11 says, "Here there is not Greek and Jew, circumcised and uncir-

---

[86] Schreiner, *Galatians*, 221.

[87] The Authorised Daily Prayer Book of the United Hebrew Congregations of the British Commonwealth of Nations, tr. S. Singer, 2nd rev. ed. (London: Eyre & Spottiswoode, 1962), 6-7 quoted in Longenecker, *Galatians*, 157.

[88] Attributed to Thales and Socrates, but also to Plato and Lactantius, quoted in Longenecker, *Galatians*, 157.

[89] Douglas Moo, *The Letters to the Colossians and to Philemon* (Grand Rapids: Eerdmans, 2008), 272.

cumcised, barbarian, Scythian, slave, free; but Christ is all, and in all." As in Galatians 3:28, we see that there is no longer a division between Jew and Greek and slave and free, but the oddball out is the reference to "Scythians." They are referred to only here in the New Testament.[90] In this time period, the Scythians corresponded to the Ethiopians at the opposite point of the compass, the distant peoples of the north. They were considered the most barbaric of barbarians, uncivilized savages, the epitome of unrefinement and savagery.[91] Josephus the Jew referred to the Scythians as little better than wild animals.[92] "Barbarian" refers to the people who live at the southern ends of the earth. So *"barbarian, Scythian"* in Colossians 3:11 refers to the peoples at the extreme north and extreme south ends of the earth. The gospel is universally inclusive. Through the gospel, God is forming a new humanity consisting of all nations of the earth. In Galatians, this has particular application to Jews and Gentiles. We see this reality gloriously taught in Ephesians 2:11-22:

> *Therefore remember that at one time you Gentiles in the flesh, called "the uncircumcision" by what is called the circumcision, which is made in the flesh by hands—remember that you were at that time separated from Christ, alienated from the commonwealth of Israel and strangers to the covenants of promise, having no hope and without God in the world. But now in Christ Jesus you who once were far off have been brought near by the blood of Christ. For*

---

[90] For this paragraph, I am dependent on Richard Bauckham, *Bible and Mission* (Grand Rapids: Baker Academic, 2003), 69-70

[91] Moo, *The Letters to the Colossians,* 271.

[92] *Contra Apion* 2.269

he himself is our peace, who has made us both one and has broken down in his flesh the dividing wall of hostility by abolishing the law of commandments expressed in ordinances, that he might create in himself one new man in place of the two, so making peace, and might reconcile us both to God in one body through the cross, thereby killing the hostility. And he came and preached peace to you who were far off and peace to those who were near. For through him we both have access in one Spirit to the Father. So then you are no longer strangers and aliens, but you are fellow citizens with the saints and members of the household of God, built on the foundation of the apostles and prophets, Christ Jesus himself being the cornerstone, in whom the whole structure, being joined together, grows into a holy temple in the Lord. In him you also are being built together into a dwelling place for God by the Spirit.

In Ephesians 3:6, Paul says, "This mystery is that the Gentiles are fellow heirs, members of the same body, and partakers of the promise in Christ Jesus through the gospel."

Now, this does not mean that all differences are erased. Paul himself, in other places, tells slaves to obey their masters and tells wives to submit to their husbands. We all keep our ethnicities and gender roles, but old divisions and wrong attitudes of superiority are abolished. These distinctions are irrelevant for being included in Christ.

29 *And if you are Christ's, then you are Abraham's offspring, heirs according to promise.*

We have already seen this truth in Galatians 3:7, but due to the rampant confusion over this teaching in the American church, it is worth pointing out each time we come across it. To limit ourselves to Galatians, Paul teaches the same truth throughout:

3:7 *Know then that it is those of faith who are the sons of Abraham.*

3:29 *And if you are Christ's, then you are Abraham's offspring, heirs according to promise.*

4:28 *Now you, brothers, like Isaac, are children of promise.*

4:31 *So, brothers, we are not children of the slave but of the free woman.*

6:16 *And as for all who walk by this rule, peace and mercy be upon them, and upon the Israel of God.*

We see that it is those who believe who are the true Israel. It is those who glory in Christ Jesus who are the circumcision (Phil 3:3). Am I saying that the church=Israel and Israel=church like Covenant Theology? No. Let's pay close attention to our text. Paul says, "If we are Christ's, then you are Abraham's offspring." As in all of theology, Christ is the key! We cannot simply equate the church and Israel. The proper theological articulation is not Israel=church, but Israel=Christ=church. We only receive the promise made to Israel by being united to the only faithful Israelite in history: Jesus. Jesus recapitulates the life of Israel.[93] He is the faithful Israelite, and all who trust in his faithfulness become Israelites *with him.* It is worth quoting Southern Baptist theologian Russell Moore at length on this point:

> For the new covenant apostles, Jew-Gentile unity is pivotal to the early church. It is about more than human relational harmony. Instead, it acknowledges that God's kingdom purposes are *in Christ.* He is the last man and the true Israel, the bearer of the Spirit. A Jewish person who clings to

[93] Russell D. Moore, "Personal and Cosmic Eschatology," in *A Theology for the Church* (Nashville: B&H Academic, 2007), 864.

the tribal markings of the old covenant acts as though the eschaton has not arrived, as though one were still waiting for the promised seed. Both Jews and Gentiles must instead see their identities not in themselves or in the flesh but in Jesus Christ and in him alone. Jesus is the descendant of Abraham, the one who deserves the throne of David. He is the obedient Israel who inherits the blessings of the Mosaic covenant. He is the propitiation of God's wrath. He is the firstborn from the dead, the resurrection and the life. Those who are in Christ—whether Jew or Gentile—receive with him all the eschatological blessing that are due to him. In him, they are all, whether Jew or Gentile, sons of God—not only in terms of relationship with the Father but also in terms of promised inheritance (Rom 8:12-17). In Christ, they all—whether Jew or Gentile—are sons of Abraham, the true circumcision, the holy nation, and the household and commonwealth of God (Gal 3:23-4:7; Eph 2-3; Col 2:6-15; 3:3-11; 1 Pet 2:9-10)... Both covenant theology and Dispensationalism, however, often discuss Israel and the church without taking into account the Christocentric nature of biblical eschatology. The future restoration of Israel has *never* been promised to the unfaithful, unregenerate members of the nation (John 3:3-10; Rom 2:25-29)—only to the faithful remnant. The church is not Israel, at least not in a direct, unmediated sense. The remnant of Israel—a biological descendant of Abraham, a circumcised Jewish firstborn son who is approved of by God for his obedience to the covenant—receives *all* of the promises due to him. Israel is Jesus of Nazareth, who, as promised to Israel, is raised from the dead and marked out with the Spirit (Ezek 37:13-14; Rom 1:2-4). ... Dispensationalists are right that only ethnic Jews receive the promised future restoration, but Paul makes clear that the "seed of Abraham" is singular, not plural (Gal 3:16). Only the circumcised can

> inherit the promised future for Israel. All believers—Jew and Greek, slave and free, male and female—are forensically Jewish firstborn sons of God (Gal 3:28). They are *in Christ*... In Christ, I inherit all the promises due to Abraham's offspring so that everything that is true of him is true of me.... The future of Israel then does belong to Gentile believers but only because they are in union with a Jewish Messiah.[94]

Interestingly (and perhaps inconsistently), Covenant Theologian Vern Poythress agrees with this point. He writes, "Because Christ is an Israelite and Christians are in union with Christ, Christians partake of the benefits promised to Israel and Judah in Jeremiah. With whom is the new covenant made? It is made with Israel and Judah. Hence it is made with Christians by virtue of Christ the Israelite."[95] The question I have for Vern is, "How can one maintain this position while remaining a paedobaptist?" If believers receive the promises of Israel by union with Christ, how can this apply to infants? Union with Christ occurs through faith. Infants can't exercise faith. It is Christ and *his* descendants who are blessed with Abraham, and Christ had no physical descendants. Jesus has no grandchildren. His descendants are *spiritual*.

I mentioned previously that whole systems of theology differ over the interpretation of this book. Let me illustrate. If I have been faithful to Paul here, then Dispensationalism cannot be true. The Bible does not make a sharp distinction

---

[94] Ibid., 867-68, 906-07.

[95] Vern Poythress, *Understanding Dispensationalism* (Phillipsburg, NJ: P&R Publishing, 1987), 106. See also p. 43 and 126.

between Israel and the church. The church is the true Israel. God promised Abraham the world (Rom 4:13), not a small piece of real estate in the East. The Bible Church movement is by and large a Dispensational denomination (although this is changing).

We also see that we can't simply equate the church and Israel. Israel was redeemed physically, but most of them were hard-hearted, or better, stiff-necked. I showed that the three-fold division of the law cannot be sustained by the Bible. I also showed that the "covenant of grace" does not do justice to the various covenants given in Scripture. Now, let's think about the implications for a moment. You will rarely hear a Covenant Theologian argue for infant baptism based on the New Testament. What do they appeal to? Covenant Theology. They try to say that Israel is no different than the church and that the new covenant is nothing more than a new administration of the covenant of grace. So, if the fundamental tenets of Covenant Theology are not biblically grounded, the whole system falls. If the system of Covenant Theology falls, then infant baptism falls for many Presbyterians. If infant baptism falls, then everyone becomes Baptist! I hope you see the staggering implications of the interpretation of this important letter. Exegesis must inform theology.

Application

- Again we see that race, class, gender, and politics should be irrelevant in the church of Jesus Christ. All are one in Christ Jesus. Here we are forced to examine our own hearts to make sure we are continually ridding ourselves of any feelings of superiority.

- We should also be aware of how some people abuse the awesome inclusivity of this passage. If there is no longer male or female, does this then mean that homosexuality is to be tolerated within the new covenant? No. This is clear in many places (1 Cor 6:9-10, Rom 1:26-27). Does it mean that gender roles should be tossed out the window, as the feminist movement says? No. We must interpret Scripture in light of Scripture. Galatians 3:28 is not the only passage in the New Testament dealing with sexuality and gender. Paul clearly teaches that men are to lead in the church and in the home (Eph 5:22-33, 1 Tim 2:11-15). Men and women are of equal essence with different roles.

New Exodus: From Slaves to Sons (4:1-7)

The law was in place for a time during the spiritual minority of God's people, but now that "faith" has come, the time set by the Father has come and Christians are to live as free and mature sons.[96]

> 1-3 *I mean that the heir, as long as he is a child, is no different from a slave, though he is the owner of everything, but he is under guardians and managers until the date set by his father. In the same way we also, when we were children, were enslaved to the elementary principles of the world.*

Paul uses another analogy to show the temporary nature of the Mosaic covenant. He is making the same point he made with the "babysitter" metaphor. The "guardians and managers" are conceptually equivalent to the babysitter. In verse three, Paul amazingly lumps together the back-

[96] Longenecker, *Galatians,* 161

grounds of both Jews and Gentiles! We will unpack the words *elemental spirits* in the next chapter.

4-5 *But when the fullness of time had come, God sent forth his Son, born of woman, born under the law, to redeem those who were under the law, so that we might receive adoption as sons.*

Notice the structure of this wonderful passage: God sent forth His Son. When? When the fullness of time had come. What about the Son? He was born of a woman; born under the law. Why? To redeem those who were under the law. Why? So that we might receive adoption as sons.

The Father sent the Son. This presupposes that the Son already existed. He has always existed.

Christ redeemed us so that we might receive adoption as sons. This idea of sonship can be traced through the canon. We first see it with Adam. In Genesis 1, Adam is not called a son of God, but he is made in the image of God, which is closely tied to sonship. We know this from Genesis 5:1-3, which says, "This is the book of the generations of Adam. When God created man, he made him in the likeness of God. Male and female he created them, and he blessed them and named them Man when they were created. When Adam had lived 130 years, he fathered a son in his own likeness, after his image, and named him Seth." Here we see that Seth is the son of Adam. Seth is made in the likeness of Adam, after his image, showing the tight relationship between image and sonship. Add to that Luke 3:38, which explicitly calls Adam the son of God. As we continue along the storyline, Israel is called Yahweh's first born son (Exod 4:22). Later still, David is told that the Lord will have a father/son relationship with his son. Second Samuel 7:13-14 says, "He shall build a house for my name, and I will establish the throne of his kingdom forever. I will be to him a father, and he shall be to me a son." In Psalm 2:7, a Davidic psalm, we read, "You are my Son; today I have begotten you." But we know that ultimately, Jesus Christ is the "capital S" Son of God. The Father tells Jesus that he is his Son, with whom he is well pleased. We become "sons" of God by being united to *the* Son of God through faith (Gal 3:26, 4:5).

> 6 *And because you are sons, God has sent the Spirit of his Son into our hearts, crying, "Abba! Father!"*

Paul now comes full circle with the Holy Spirit (See Gal 3:2, 14). The old era is over. The coming of the Messiah and the Spirit show that the new age is here. Why are you turning back? Don't go back to the age of Adam; the age without the Spirit; don't return to the babysitter; don't go back to the elemental spirits, guardians, and managers. God has sent his Spirit, and his Son to redeem us from the present evil age (Gal 1:4). The new creation has come (Gal 6:15)!

With the language of redemption and the Spirit, Paul is probably referring to the hope of a second exodus.[97] Isaiah 48:16-17 says, "Draw near to me, hear this: from the beginning I have not spoken in secret, from the time it came to be I have been there. And now the Lord GOD has sent me, and his Spirit. Thus says the LORD, your Redeemer, the Holy One of Israel: 'I am the LORD your God, who teaches you to profit, who leads you in the way you should go.'"

Here we also have a clear reference to the Trinity. We see that the Son and the Spirit are on the same plane be-

---

[97] Schreiner, *Galatians*, 237.

cause they are both sent by the Father. God the Father sends the Spirit of the Son. First Corinthians 12:4-6 is another clearly Trinitarian passage: *"Now there are varieties of gifts, but the same Spirit; and there are varieties of service, but the same Lord; and there are varieties of activities, but it is the same God who empowers them all in everyone."* As with all God's actions, the work is from the Father, through the Son, by the Spirit.[98]

Abba is the Aramaic term for Father. It is a term of love and endearment to be sure—but probably not Daddy, as is popular among preachers.[99] "Father" is the translational equivalent of *Abba.*[100] It is the term Jesus used to refer to the Father.

> *7 So you are no longer a slave, but a son, and if a son, then an heir through God.*

Christ has redeemed us. We have been changed from slaves to sons. Indeed, even heirs! We see a similar truth taught in Romans 8:15-17: "For you did not receive the spirit of slavery to fall back into fear, but you have received the Spirit of adoption as sons, by whom we cry, 'Abba! Father!' The Spirit himself bears witness with our spirit that we are children of God, and if children, then heirs—heirs of God and fellow heirs with Christ, provided we suffer with him in order that we may also be glorified with him."

---

[98] Robert Letham, *The Holy Trinity* (Phillipsburg, NJ: P&R Publishing, 2004), 413.

[99] Ibid., 37

[100] Gordon Fee, *God's Empowering Presence* (Peabody, MA: Hendrickson, 1994), 412.

Application

- J.I. Packer calls adoption "the highest privilege that the gospel offers."[101] Sometimes an overemphasis on the legal metaphor (justification) can produce a mechanical relationship with the Lord, but adoption is a familial and relational term.[102] It conveys closeness, affection, and generosity. We are loved and cared for by God our Father. We are transferred from one family to another. We are no longer *sons* of disobedience (Eph 2:2) or *children* of wrath (Eph 2:3), but have been given a new name, a new status, and a new identity. We are now part of a new household (Gal 6:10, Eph 2:19). As proof that we are sons, God has given us his Spirit. So the Spirit is called the Spirit of adoption (Rom 8:15). We are born again, born from above into a new family. As Alister McGrath writes, "Adoption is about *being wanted.* It is about *belonging.* These are deeply emotive themes, which resonate with the cares and concerns of many in our increasingly fractured society. To be adopted is to be invited into a loving and caring environment. It is about being welcomed, wanted and invited. Adoption celebrates the privilege of invitation, in which the outsider is welcomed into the fold of faith

---

[101] J.I. Packer, *Knowing God* (Downers Grove, IVP, 1973), 206.

[102] Trevor J. Burke, *Adopted into God's Family. NSBT* (Downers Grove, IL: IVP, 2006), 194.

and love."[103] Just like most things in the Christian life, there is an already/not yet tension with adoption. We are adopted, but we await final adoption (Rom 8:23), the redemption of our bodies. Then we will be finally and fully conformed to the image of God's unique Son, Jesus (Rom 8:29). First John 3:1-2 says, "See what kind of love the Father has given to us, that we should be called children of God; and so we are. The reason why the world does not know us is that it did not know him. Beloved, we are God's children now, and what we will be has not yet appeared; but we know that when he appears we shall be like him, because we shall see him as he is." As sons, we should expect God's care, but also his discipline, because he loves his children, and those whom he loves, he disciplines (Heb 12:7-11).

- Christians should model the love of God by pursuing adoption themselves. There are thousands of children in need of loving, godly parents. What an opportunity for missions! We often forget that our closest and primary mission field lives within our walls. Our children need to be nurtured in the gospel. There are orphans all over the world in need of homes. Adopting unwanted children is a fantastic way to model God's adopting love. Christian

---

[103] Alister McGrath, *Knowing Christ* (London: Hodder & Stoughton, 2001), 144-45 quoted in Burke, *Adopted into God's Family,* 197.

churches should be full of people who are seeking to adopt neglected children. Who else will?[104]

[104] See Russell Moore, *Adopted for Life* (Wheaton, IL: Crossway, 2009).

Chapter 8
Galatians 4:8-20

Passage

Formerly, when you did not know God, you were enslaved to those that by nature are not gods. But now that you have come to know God, or rather to be known by God, how can you turn back again to the weak and worthless elementary principles of the world, whose slaves you want to be once more? You observe days and months and seasons and years! I am afraid I may have labored over you in vain. Brothers, I entreat you, become as I am, for I also have become as you are. You did me no wrong. You know it was because of a bodily ailment that I preached the gospel to you at first, and though my condition was a trial to you, you did not scorn or despise me, but received me as an angel of God, as Christ Jesus. What then has become of the blessing you felt? For I testify to you that, if possible, you would have gouged out your eyes and given them to me. Have I then become your enemy by telling you the truth? They make much of you, but for no good purpose. They want to shut you out, that you may make much of them. It is always good to be made much of for a good purpose, and not only when I am present with you, my little children, for whom I am again in the anguish of childbirth until Christ is formed in you! I wish I could be present with you now and change my tone, for I am perplexed about you.

Don't Turn Back! (4:8-11)

8 *Formerly, when you did not know God, you were enslaved to those that by nature are not gods.*

Formerly, you were slaves. You were enslaved to those that by nature are not gods. Jews and Gentiles had drastically different backgrounds, but Paul thinks of both as times of *enslavement*.

What are "those that are by nature, not gods?" Clearly, they are false gods, idols. We are helped in our understanding of this truth by looking at the book of 1 Corinthians. There, referring to idols, Paul says "there may be so-called gods in heaven or on earth—as indeed there are many 'gods' and many 'lords'" (8:5). Then in 10:20 he says that these idols are demons: "No, I imply that what pagans sacrifice they offer to demons and not to God." Paul's understanding of idols is complex.[105] On the one hand, they are nothing—not gods. Yet, on the other hand, one must be careful because behind these false gods, these idols, lies demonic activity.

> 9 *But now that you have come to know God, or rather to be known by God, how can you turn back again to the weak and worthless elementary principles of the world, whose slaves you want to be once more?*

Paul is absolutely committed to the priority of grace. He begins with a statement which might give room for human credit, but he is quick to correct himself here. It is not that you know God, but that you are known *by God.* God is always the initiator. Paul is jealous to keep people from getting the glory that only God deserves. We saw this in the beginning of the letter when he wrote, "to whom be the glory forever and ever. Amen" (Gal 1:5). We know God, not because we had the insight to find him, but because he first knows us. Praise him!

He continues, asking the Galatians, "Now that you are known by the living God, how can you turn back to the

---

105 See Christopher Wright, *The Mission of God* (Downers Grove, IL: IVP, 2006), 136-188.

weak and worthless elemental spirits (*stoichēia*)?" This is strong language. Think through it carefully with me. The Galatians were being urged to return to the law covenant. The Judaizers were trying to enslave them by making them obey the law for justification (Gal 2:4). Paul could have said, "Why do you want to return to the old covenant law?", but instead he says, "Why are you turning back to the weak and worthless elemental spirits whose slaves you want to be once more?" To return to the law after the coming of the Messiah is to return to their pagan, idolatrous background, which is to return to the elemental spirits.

So the all-important question for this passage is, "What did Paul mean by 'weak and worthless elemental spirits'?" From verse eight, we already see that it is closely tied to their pagan backgrounds (you were enslaved to those that by nature are not gods), and we see from both 8 and 9 that they enslave. Paul previously used this word in Galatians 4:3: "*In the same way we also, when we were children, were enslaved to the elementary principles of the world*." Here Paul says "we!" He sees his own past in Judaism as equivalent to the elemental spirits of the world. This is radical.

The phrase *elemental spirits* can refer to one of two things.[106] Either it means the basic building blocks of the world or demonic forces. For this author, context weighs heavily in favor of a reference to demonic forces, or what

---

106 There are obviously more than these two interpretations of this word. Most will fit into one of these two broad categories. See any commentary on Galatians or Colossians for more information.

Paul calls "principalities and powers" elsewhere.[107] The ESV translates the word *elementary principles* here, but translates the same word *elemental spirits* in Colossians:

> Colossians 2:8 *See to it that no one takes you captive by philosophy and empty deceit, according to human tradition, according to the elemental spirits of the world, and not according to Christ.*
>
> *Colossians 2:20 If with Christ you died to the elemental spirits of the world, why, as if you were still alive in the world, do you submit to regulations—*

Even if one opts for the "building blocks" view, in the end, spiritual forces can't be excluded. For, unlike the mindset of Enlightenment rationalism, in the mindset of the New Testament the "whole world lies in the power of the evil one" (1 John 5:19). Satan is the "god of this world" (2 Cor 4:4). He is the "ruler of this world" (John 12:31). Unbelievers follow "the prince of the power of the air" (Eph 2:2). There are cosmic powers, spiritual forces of evil over this present darkness (Eph 6:12). So even if the word does refer to the elementary building blocks of the world, demonic forces are inevitably involved.

The genitive "*of the world*" (*tou kosmou*) is important and lends toward a demonic element as well. These elemental spirits are characteristic of this world, this age, which he already wrote is evil (Gal 1:4). This present world order belongs to Satan (2 Cor 4:4) and his minions.

---

[107] Clinton E. Arnold, "Returning to the Domain of the Powers: *stoicheia* as Evil Spirits in Galatians 4:3, 9," *Novum Testamentum* 38, no. 1 (January 1996): 57; idem, *Powers of Darkness: Principalities and Powers in Paul's Letters* (Downers Grove, IL: InterVarsity Press, 1992), 53, 131-32.

10-11 *You observe days and months and seasons and years! I am afraid I may have labored over you in vain.*

To me, this is one of Paul's most radical statements.[108] In the preceding verses, he speaks of the Galatians' returning to their pagan backgrounds, with its lords that cannot liberate. He speaks of returning to the elemental spirits of the world. Then in verse 10, he tells us what he is referring to: observing days, months, seasons, and years. Unbelievable! The Sabbath is obviously included in these observances. Here, Paul says that observing the Sabbath and other such Jewish observances required by the law is equivalent to paganism! After the coming of Christ, to return to the law is to return to paganism.[109] It is to return to being enslaved to those that are by nature not gods, which is another way of saying being enslaved by the elemental spirits of this present evil age.

It's important to note that Paul is not calling the law demonic in and of itself here. However, it is demonic to return to the law for justification *after* Christ's death and

---

[108] Longenecker writes, "Beyond question, Paul's lumping of Judaism and paganism together in this manner is radical in the extreme," *Galatians,* 181.

[109] Tom Schreiner writes, "One of the most surprising themes of this section becomes clear here. Paul compares devotion to the Mosaic law to reverting to paganism. The Galatians before their conversion to Christ were devoted to false gods (4:8), and yet Paul sees their attraction to Judaism as equivalent to paganism," in *Galatians,* 245.

resurrection.[110] Christ is the end of the law for righteousness to all who believe (Rom 10:4). Its sacrifices are no longer effective. To turn back the clock of redemptive history is to turn back to slavery to the powers.

Paul fears for his fellow believers. He has worked to nourish their faith and they are in danger of throwing it out the window. To seek salvation in anything other than Christ crucified is to fall from grace (Gal 5:4).

Application

- Rest in God's electing love. You know him because he first knew you (4:9). The doctrine of election tends to be a controversial doctrine, but it should not be. It should be a warm blanket for the cold soul. How liberating it is to know God's sovereign and effective grace. Rest in it.
- If my interpretation is correct, it just reinforces the fact that getting the gospel right is crucial. It is fundamentally demonic to trust in anything but Christ crucified for salvation. This is why John can call

---

110 Richard Longenecker writes that Paul's use of the adverbs *anew* and *again* in Gal 4:9 "emphasizes the fact that by taking on Torah observance Gentile Christians would be reverting to a pre-Christian stance comparable to their former pagan worship. ...not, of course, that paganism and the Mosaic law are qualitatively the same, but that both fall under the same judgment when seen from the perspective of being 'in Christ' and that both come under the same condemnation when favored above Christ. Beyond question, Paul's lumping of Judaism and paganism together in this manner is radical in the extreme," *Galatians,* 181.

those who falsely claim to be Jews "the synagogue of Satan" (Rev 2:9, 3:9). In this regard the principalities and powers can equally plunder the Roman Catholic Church or the overly strict fundamentalist Baptist congregation. The "do this and live" principle is everywhere because the main evangelist of this religion is the prince of the power of the air. It is demonic to trust in yourself. In Acts 21:24, the verbal form (*stoicheō*) is used of "live in observance of the law." In Colossae, there were intruders trying to force the Colossians to live a certain way with regard to food, drink, festivals and Sabbaths (Col 2:16). They were insisting on asceticism (Col 2:18). They were all about rules. But we have died to the law (Rom 7:4) and have died to the elemental spirits of the world (Col 2:20). We are no longer required to "submit to regulations—do not handle, do not taste, do not touch" (Col 2:20-21). Verlyn Verbrugge writes, "Thus 'the basic principles of the world' cover all the things in which humans place trust apart from the living God revealed in Christ."[111] William Hendricksen defines the elemental spirits as "elementary teachings regarding rules and regulations, by means of which, before Christ's coming, people,

---

[111] Verlyn D. Verbrugge, ed., *New International Dictionary of New Testament Theology: Abridged Edition* (Grand Rapids: Zondervan, 2000), 541. Longenecker writes similarly, "For Paul, however, whatever leads one away from sole reliance on Christ, whether based on good intentions or depraved desires, is sub-Christian and therefore to be condemned," *Galatians*, 181.

both Jews and Gentiles, each in their own way, attempted by their own efforts, and in accordance with the promptings of their own fleshly (unregenerate) nature, to achieve salvation."[112]

- This perspective is also clear from Philippians 3:2. The Judaizers were very concerned about being ceremonially clean, doing good, and being circumcised, and Paul provocatively calls them dogs (unclean), evil doers (opposite of good), and those who mutilate the flesh (*tēn katatōmēn*). He is saying that those who cut themselves thinking this will gain salvation are "like the frenzied prophets of Baal who were frustrated that their god would not answer their pleas" (see 1 Kin 18:28, Lev 19:28, 21:5 LXX).[113] They are acting like pagans. So don't try to be good to be saved. Don't insist on adding to the gospel with rules. Don't worship a false god. Such behavior is fundamentally demonic.
- From this passage we see that we all have the same past. Some of us had very immoral lives before coming to Christ. Some of us grew up in moral homes. The common denominator of all these is the elemental spirits. No matter where we come from, before coming to Christ we are enslaved under the elemental spirits of the world.

---

[112] William Hendricksen, *Exposition of Galatians* (Grand Rapids: Baker Book House, 1979), 157.

[113] Frank Thielman, *Theology of the New Testament* (Grand Rapids: Zondervan, 2005), 318; Wright, *Justification,* 142.

- We also see that we were and are all worshippers. Worship is not an activity, but an identity. It is inevitable. The Galatians were not free before they came to Christ, because *no one* is free. People often say they dislike Christianity because they prefer their freedom. "I will be ruled by none" they proclaim. Satan loves to deceive people in this way. Everyone is a slave, either to sin or to righteousness. Slavery to sin can manifest itself in many ways: family, career, money, relationships, image—something will be your lord. Behind all idols lies demonic activity—Islam, atheism, materialism, hedonism, agnosticism, Latter Day Saints, or Roman Catholicism. Any system that teaches or assumes a person can be saved by one's own efforts has the Prince of Darkness as its founder. The elemental spirits are the "A,B,C's" of man-made religion—you do, therefore you get. The thought that obedience leads to blessing is the most popular religious belief of our day, but it is fundamentally *wrong*.
- The principalities and powers desire to have you focus your life on anything other than Christ. They will use anything they can: addiction, family, religion, politics. Often in the lives of Christians, they will use good things to distract us from the great thing. They want to make good things become "god things" in our lives. Christian, beware of the decep-

tiveness of false gods.[114] Always strive to keep Christ central, where he belongs.

You Know Who I Am: Personal Appeals (4:12-20)

Here, we begin the practical application of Paul's self-defense and his theological defense.

> 12 *Brothers, I entreat you, become as I am, for I also have become as you are. You did me no wrong.*

In some ways, this is the summary statement of the whole letter: Become like me by being free from the law, just as I have become like you. It is also very important to point out that this is the first imperative of the letter. Paul did not start the letter by simply bossing them around and telling them what to do. He didn't say, "You guys need to be doing this, this, and that." No, he begins with theology, and lots of it, four and a half chapters of it. He lays out his apostolic authority, the doctrine of justification by faith and not by works of the law, the centrality of Christ crucified, the reception of the Spirit, and the role of the law in redemptive history before he starts morally instructing the Galatians.

Martin Luther writes, "Up till now Paul has been occupied wholly in teaching. He is so incensed at the Galatians' revolt that he calls them fools, bewitched, not believing the truth, crucifiers of Christ, and so on. Having finished most of his letter, he begins to realize that he has treated them too sharply. Therefore, being careful not to do more harm

---

[114] See Tim Keller's *Counterfeit Gods: The Empty Promises of Money, Sex, and Power, and the Only Hope That Matters* (New York: Dutton, 2009).

than good, he shows that his sharp chiding came from fatherly affection and a true apostolic heart. No doubt many people were offended by his words, but he qualifies the matter with gentle words to win them back."[115]

> 13–16 *You know it was because of a bodily ailment that I preached the gospel to you at first, and though my condition was a trial to you, you did not scorn or despise me, but received me as an angel of God, as Christ Jesus. What then has become of the blessing you felt? For I testify to you that, if possible, you would have gouged out your eyes and given them to me. Have I then become your enemy by telling you the truth?*

Paul's simple point is that they can trust him. They used to be friends. They welcomed him and his teaching before. "Did you forget what I did for you in preaching the gospel? Do you remember how blessed it was?"

Sickness and disease is off-putting but it wasn't a stumbling block for the Galatians' reception of Paul. They received him as an angel, as Christ Jesus himself. How could they turn on him and his teaching so quickly?

Although we should rarely speculate, some see in this verse an allusion to Paul's thorn in the flesh. They think that Paul had a problem with his eyes. Here Paul says the Galatians were even willing to gouge out their eyes and give them to Paul. This could simply be hyperbole to show how much love they previously had for the apostle since the eyes are very core organs and the Galatians were willing to depart with them for their apostle. Also, in Galatians 6:11, Paul says that he is writing with his own hands in large letters. This may have something to do with his eye-

---

[115] Luther, *Galatians,* 218.

sight, but it may not. The fact is Paul never tells us what the thorn was, so we ought to be silent where Scripture is silent.

> 17-19 *They make much of you, but for no good purpose. They want to shut you out, that you may make much of them. It is always good to be made much of for a good purpose, and not only when I am present with you, my little children, for whom I am again in the anguish of childbirth until Christ is formed in you!*

Paul insists that the agitators are not out for their best interest. They are actually after their own interest. They want to shut them out of the people of God so that they will become their own people. They want to be exalted. Paul's goal, on the other hand, is that Christ be formed in them. Paul is truly after their good, which is also for God's glory. In 1 Corinthians 4:15, he says, *"For though you have countless guides in Christ, you do not have many fathers. For I became your father in Christ Jesus through the gospel."*

> 20 *I wish I could be present with you now and change my tone, for I am perplexed about you.*

Paul's preference would be to be with them face to face. It is hard to read tone in letters. Paul wants to sit with them, sing with them, and pray with them. He loves the Galatians and wants to restore them to the true gospel so that Christ will receive his rightful glory. He is perplexed about what they are doing: "How could you be so confused? You know me. You know what I have been through. You know my history and how I related to the Jerusalem apostles. You have heard how I had to confront Peter. You know that a person is justified by faith in Christ and not by works of the law. Don't you remember? You received the Holy Spirit. Did you forget? How could you? Remember that you received him by faith—not by works of the law. Remember the story of the Hebrew Scriptures? Remember that the law was given 430 years after the promise was made to Abraham. Isn't it clear? The law was not designed to give life. Life only comes through Christ. The law just says 'do' and therefore curses because no one can obey it. The law was temporary, a babysitter put in place until we matured. We were minors under the law but have matured to full grown sons now. Don't go back. How could you want to be enslaved all over again? I am perplexed."

Application

- We see that for Paul doctrine really matters. That means it should matter to us. Paul loves the Galatians and has a strong desire to correct their thinking with the gospel. It is not that Paul simply wants them to believe the same things he does (though that is true), but Paul knows that right thinking leads to right living just as wrong thinking leads to wrong living. Doctrine is the stuff of life.
- We should be in the pains of childbirth for our children and our fellow church members until Christ is formed in them. When you see a fellow believer fall into sin, don't walk away criticizing them in your heart. Don't be self-righteous, but pray that the Lord would cause you pain when you see sin in your fellow believers. Pray for them. Confront them when necessary, for their good.
- The servants of the gospel will suffer in this age, as Paul did. This has always been the case, although you won't hear much about it in contemporary church growth books. Tertullian said long ago that

the blood of the martyrs is the seed of the church. Suffering is the way God works with his people. He is that *kind* of God.

- Always make the gospel the foundation for instruction, as Paul did here. He laid out his history and the nature of his apostolic office, justification, the Spirit, and the law in redemptive history before he starts morally instructing the Galatians.

Chapter 9: Galatians 4:21-5:1

Tell me, you who desire to be under the law, do you not listen to the law? For it is written that Abraham had two sons, one by a slave woman and one by a free woman. But the son of the slave was born according to the flesh, while the son of the free woman was born through promise. Now this may be interpreted allegorically: these women are two covenants. One is from Mount Sinai, bearing children for slavery; she is Hagar. Now Hagar is Mount Sinai in Arabia; she corresponds to the present Jerusalem, for she is in slavery with her children. But the Jerusalem above is free, and she is our mother. For it is written, "Rejoice, O barren one who does not bear; break forth and cry aloud, you who are not in labor! For the children of the desolate one will be more than those of the one who has a husband." Now you, brothers, like Isaac, are children of promise. But just as at that time he who was born according to the flesh persecuted him who was born according to the Spirit, so also it is now. But what does the Scripture say? "Cast out the slave woman and her son, for the son of the slave woman shall not inherit with the son of the free woman." So, brothers, we are not children of the slave but of the free woman. For freedom Christ has set us free; stand firm therefore, and do not submit again to a yoke of slavery.

At this point, we need to remind ourselves where we have been. Paul began the letter by defending his apostleship. He was being accused of being dependent upon the Jerusalem apostles and of distorting their message. This is why he begins the letter: "Paul, an apostle—not from men nor through man, but through Jesus Christ" (Gal 1:1). His gospel was not a human gospel. He received it "through a revelation of Jesus Christ" (Gal 1:12). He didn't distort the message, but received the "right hand of fellowship" from the Jerusalem pillars (Gal 2:9). He even had to confront the apostle Peter because his "conduct was not in step with the truth of the gospel" (Gal 2:14). Peter should have known that a person is not justified by works of the law but through faith in Jesus Christ (Gal 2:16). All flesh will not be justified by works of the law.[116] The Galatians had received the gift of the promised Holy Spirit by faith and not by works of the law. How could they be so confused? How could they return to the law, which only demands and never gives? Those who try to follow its demands fail to and end up cursed (Gal 3:10-14). Then Paul lays out the purpose of the law in God's plan. It was given as a temporary babysitter 430 years after the promise to Abraham (Gal 3:17) until the Messiah. It was never designed to give life (Gal 3:21). It was put in charge as a nanny until Christ, the true seed of Abraham (Gal 3:16), came. Now, all who trust the Messiah are united to him and are therefore children of Abraham as well (Gal 3:28-29). We are no longer minors but mature sons (Gal 4:1-7). To return to the law covenant is to return to paganism; it is to return to being enslaved under the elemental spirits of the world. How could the Galatians forget all of this and forget their relationship with Paul (Gal 4:12-20)? This brings us to our present section.

Change of Tone: We are Children of the Free Woman (4:21-31)

Richard Longenecker points out four central points to keep in mind when dealing with this Sarah/Hagar allegory:

---

[116] My literal translation of Galatians 2:16.

1. The central question dealt with by Paul is: Who are Abraham's true children?

2. Paul is using the Hagar-Sarah allegory in an *ad hominem* fashion (arguing against the opponents—"to the man") and this approach must be seen in that light. It is not his normal way of teaching.

3. Paul's message is specific here. He is arguing against Judaizers, not Christian Jews in general.

4. This story is an explanation of his overall exhortation in 4:12: Become like me![117]

Introduction (21-23)[118]

> 21 *Tell me, you who desire to be under the law, do you not listen to the law?*

It is not simply that they want to be circumcised—no, they want to be under the law. Jews viewed the law as a unit. There was no tripartite distinction of the law in the first century. That is a later theological construction. To seek to be circumcised and to observe days, months, and years was to desire to be under the whole law. Paul has been showing them from the law that they should not seek justification through the law. He is challenging them to really hear the law. If they would listen to the law, they would not be returning to the law.

Earlier, I mentioned how for Paul, to be *under* law (Gal 4:5, 4:21, 5:18) is equivalent to:

- Being under a curse (Gal 3:10)

---

[117] Longenecker, *Galatians* 219.

[118] Meyer points out this literary structure in *The End of the Law,* 116; so also Schreiner, *Galatians,* 264.

- Being under sin (Gal 3:22)
- Being under a babysitter (Gal 3:24)
- Being under guardians and managers (Gal 4:2)
- Being enslaved under the elemental spirits (Gal 4:3)

22-23 *For it is written that Abraham had two sons, one by a slave woman and one by a free woman. But the son of the slave was born according to the flesh, while the son of the free woman was born through promise.*

Do you remember the story in Genesis? The opponents may have used this passage to support their arguments, but at the end of the day we are not sure.[119] Sarah suggested that Abraham sleep with Hagar to produce an heir, and she gave birth to Ishmael. Sarah's attempt at children was fleshly.[120] Sarah's children were the result of divine intervention.[121] Abraham was 100 years old after all. As we have seen, flesh characterizes human desires and sin. Promise is the opposite of flesh; promise comes from God. Flesh is our fallen human nature working in its own natural strength—characteristic of the present age. The Spirit, on the other hand, inaugurates the age to come.

Construction (24-27)

24-25—*Now this may be interpreted allegorically: these women are two covenants. One is from Mount Sinai, bearing children for slavery; she is Hagar. Now Hagar is Mount Sinai in Arabia; she corresponds to the present Jerusalem, for she is in slavery with her children.*

---

[119] Longenecker, *Galatians,* 210.

[120] So the TNIV says, "through human effort."

[121] The TNIV has "as a result of a divine promise."

This word *"allegorically"* (*allēgoreō*) only occurs here in the New Testament. It is formed from two words and means "I say something else."[122] Luther writes, "If Paul had not proved the righteousness of faith against the righteousness of works by strong and pithy arguments, he would hardly have prevailed with this allegory. But because he had already strengthened his case with invincible arguments from experience, from the example of Abraham, and from the witness of Scripture, he now adds an allegory to give beauty to all the rest. It is seemly sometimes to add an allegory when the foundation has been properly laid and the matter thoroughly proved; as a painting is an ornament to decorate a house already built, so is an allegory the light of a matter that is already otherwise proved and confirmed."[123]

These women are two covenants: the old and new.[124] Hagar clearly represents the old covenant because Paul says she is from Mount Sinai. Some interpreters think the two covenants contrasted are the old covenant and the Abrahamic covenant. As we have seen though, one should not press the discontinuity too far. There is more continuity between the Abrahamic covenant and the new covenant than there is between the old covenant and the new. In Jeremiah's prophecy of a new covenant, he explicitly says that the new covenant will not be "like the covenant that I made

---

[122] Meyer, *The End of the Law*, 116.

[123] Luther, *Galatians*, 228.

[124] The majority of commentators take this view: (*e.g.*, Longenecker, *Galatians*, 211; Schreiner, *Galatians*, 269; Fee, *God's Empowering Presence*, 413, 416).

with their fathers on the day when I took them by the hand bring them out of the land of Egypt, my covenant that they broke" (Jer 31:32). The Abrahamic covenant is fulfilled in the new covenant. There is discontinuity as well though. The easiest example to point to in Galatians is circumcision. One cannot simply equate the Abrahamic and the new covenant. Circumcision clearly does not carry over. Jason Meyer writes, "The salvation-historical appearance of the new Jerusalem mirrors the establishment of the new covenant. Because the two entities are eschatologically established together as fulfillments and replacements of their former counterparts, they conceptually belong together in the nexus of redemptive history. Therefore, the eschatological contrast between the 'present' and 'above' Jerusalems suggests an eschatological contrast between the two covenants to which they correspond."[125]

"Present" Jerusalem takes us back to the earlier reference to the "present" evil age (Gal 1:4).[126] Present Jerusalem is in physical *and* spiritual slavery. The Jews were still in exile.[127] They weren't ruling, but were being ruled. They were under the thumb of the Romans. The physical slavery was a result of their spiritual slavery (see Gal 4:8-9, 5:1).

26 *But the Jerusalem above is free, and she is our mother.*

The Jerusalem above replaces earthly Jerusalem just as the new covenant replaces the old covenant. The only Jeru-

---

[125] Meyer, *The End of the Law,* 128. See 128ff for six reasons why we should see these two covenants as the old and the new.

[126] Ibid., 129.

[127] See N.T. Wright, *The New Testament and the People of God* (Minneapolis: Fortress Press, 1992).

salem that has significance in God's scheme now is the Jerusalem above. Revelation 21:2 says, "And I saw the holy city, new Jerusalem, coming down out of heaven from God." Hebrews 12:22-24 says, "But you have come to Mount Zion and to the city of the living God, the heavenly Jerusalem, and to innumerable angels in festal gathering, and to the assembly of the firstborn who are enrolled in heaven, and to God, the judge of all, and to the spirits of the righteous made perfect, and to Jesus, the mediator of a new covenant, and to the sprinkled blood that speaks a better word than the blood of Abel."

This New Jerusalem is our mother. We are the children of the new creation—the Judaizers are of the old creation. We are the people of the future. Tom Schreiner writes, "The Jerusalem above, according to Paul, is the eschatological Jerusalem that has reached down into the present evil age, so we have an example here of Paul's "already but not yet" eschatology. It also seems likely that Paul believed that the arrival of the Jerusalem above reflects an inauguration and partial fulfillment of the new covenant promise of a new creation (Isa 65:17, 66:1)."[128]

> 27 *For it is written, "Rejoice, O barren one who does not bear; break forth and cry aloud, you who are not in labor! For the children of the desolate one will be more than those of the one who has a husband."*

Often when the New Testament quotes the Old Testament, the writers are not simply appealing to a single verse but to the larger context within which that particular verse is found. Here Paul quotes Isaiah 54:1. Remember that

---

[128] Schreiner, *Galatians*, 272.

chapters 40-66 of Isaiah contain the "gospel of the Old Testament." God is promising to do a new work among his people. It will be helpful for us to look at Isaiah 53:10-55:5 to get a feel for the larger context of which this passage is found:

> *Yet it was the will of the LORD to crush him; he has put him to grief; when his soul makes an offering for guilt, he shall see his offspring; he shall prolong his days; the will of the LORD shall prosper in his hand. Out of the anguish of his soul he shall see and be satisfied; by his knowledge shall the righteous one, my servant, make many to be accounted righteous, and he shall bear their iniquities. Therefore I will divide him a portion with the many, and he shall divide the spoil with the strong, because he poured out his soul to death and was numbered with the transgressors; yet he bore the sin of many, and makes intercession for the transgressors. "Sing, O barren one, who did not bear; break forth into singing and cry aloud, you who have not been in labor! For the children of the desolate one will be more than the children of her who is married," says the LORD. "Enlarge the place of your tent, and let the curtains of your habitations be stretched out; do not hold back; lengthen your cords and strengthen your stakes. For you will spread abroad to the right and to the left, and your offspring will possess the nations and will people the desolate cities. "Fear not, for you will not be ashamed; be not confounded, for you will not be disgraced; for you will forget the shame of your youth, and the reproach of your widowhood you will remember no more. For your Maker is your husband, the LORD of hosts is his name; and the Holy One of Israel is your Redeemer, the God of the whole earth he is called. For the LORD has called you like a wife deserted and grieved in spirit, like a wife of youth when she is cast off, says your God. For a brief moment I deserted you, but with great compassion I will gather you. In overflowing anger for a moment I hid my face from you, but with everlasting love I will have compassion on you," says the LORD, your Redeemer. "This is like the days of Noah to me: as I swore that the waters of Noah*

should no more go over the earth, so I have sworn that I will not be angry with you, and will not rebuke you. For the mountains may depart and the hills be removed, but my steadfast love shall not depart from you, and my covenant of peace shall not be removed," says the LORD, who has compassion on you. "O afflicted one, storm-tossed and not comforted, behold, I will set your stones in antimony, and lay your foundations with sapphires. I will make your pinnacles of agate, your gates of carbuncles, and all your wall of precious stones. All your children shall be taught by the LORD, and great shall be the peace of your children. In righteousness you shall be established; you shall be far from oppression, for you shall not fear; and from terror, for it shall not come near you. If anyone stirs up strife, it is not from me; whoever stirs up strife with you shall fall because of you. Behold, I have created the smith who blows the fire of coals and produces a weapon for its purpose. I have also created the ravager to destroy; no weapon that is fashioned against you shall succeed, and you shall confute every tongue that rises against you in judgment. This is the heritage of the servants of the LORD and their vindication from me, declares the LORD. Come, everyone who thirsts, come to the waters; and he who has no money, come, buy and eat! Come, buy wine and milk without money and without price. Why do you spend your money for that which is not bread, and your labor for that which does not satisfy? Listen diligently to me, and eat what is good, and delight yourselves in rich food. Incline your ear, and come to me; hear, that your soul may live; and I will make with you an everlasting covenant, my steadfast, sure love for David. Behold, I made him a witness to the peoples, a leader and commander for the peoples. Behold, you shall call a nation that you do not know, and a nation that did not know you shall run to you, because of the LORD your God, and of the Holy One of Israel, for he has glorified you.

Moises Silva writes, "Since Isa. 54:1 follows immediately upon the 'song' of the Suffering Servant (no doubt alluded to in Gal. 2:20-21, 3:1, 13), Paul evidently expected the Galatians to see the connection between faith in the crucified Christ and incorporation into the numerous people who have the new Jerusalem as their mother."[129] "Isaiah, then, conceived of the ideal future for which he and all God's faithful people longed, in terms of a covenant of peace that would be the culmination of all that was promised in the covenants that had marked Israel's history from the very beginning. The sacrifice of the suffering servant will be the basis of this covenant of peace."[130]

Application of the Allegory (28-31)

28 *Now you, brothers, like Isaac, are children of promise.*

The Galatians are Isaac-like because they were born spiritually and supernaturally. They are God's children by an act of God's gracious and miraculous power, not human effort. Those of faith are children of the new covenant, new creation, and new exodus.

> 29-30 *But just as at that time he who was born according to the flesh persecuted him who was born according to the Spirit, so also it is now. But what does the Scripture say? "Cast out the slave woman and her son, for the son of the slave woman shall not inherit with the son of the free woman."*

We would expect Paul to say that Isaac was born "according to promise," but he says "according to the Spirit," for Paul sees the promise and the Spirit as being bound together. The Holy Spirit is the *promised* Holy Spirit. We saw this in Galatians 3:14: [Christ redeemed us] *so that in*

---

[129] Moises Silva, "Galatians," in *Commentary on the New Testament Use of the Old Testament* (Grand Rapids: Baker, 2007), 809.

[130] Barry Webb, *The Message of Isaiah* (Downers Grove, IL: IVP, 1996), 215.

Christ Jesus the blessing of Abraham might come to the Gentiles, so that we might receive the promised Spirit through faith. Ishmael, on the other hand, was born according to flesh because Abraham and Sarah took matters into their own hands to produce a child. God works according to the Spirit and sinners depend on the flesh.[131]

We already saw the flesh/Spirit contrast in Galatians 3:3: "Are you so foolish? Having begun by the Spirit, are you now being perfected by the flesh?" and will see it again in chapter 5.[132] These themes are similar to the themes found in another very well-known Pauline new covenant passage, 2 Corinthians 3:

> *Are we beginning to commend ourselves again? Or do we need, as some do, letters of recommendation to you, or from you? You yourselves are our letter of recommendation, written on our hearts, to be known and read by all. And you show that you are a letter from Christ delivered by us, written not with ink but with the Spirit of the living God, not on tablets of stone but on tablets of human hearts. Such is the confidence that we have through Christ toward God. Not that we are sufficient in ourselves to claim anything as coming from us, but our sufficiency is from God, who has made us competent to be ministers of a new covenant, not of the letter but of the Spirit. For the letter kills, but the Spirit gives life. Now if the ministry of death, carved in letters on stone, came with such glory that the Israelites could not gaze at Moses' face because of its glory, which was being brought to an end, will not the ministry of the*

---

[131] Silva, *Galatians*, 808.

[132] Galatians 5:17 says, "For the desires of the flesh are against the Spirit, and the desires of the Spirit are against the flesh, for these are opposed to each other, to keep you from doing the things you want to do."

> *Spirit have even more glory? For if there was glory in the ministry of condemnation, the ministry of righteousness must far exceed it in glory. Indeed, in this case, what once had glory has come to have no glory at all, because of the glory that surpasses it. For if what was being brought to an end came with glory, much more will what is permanent have glory. Since we have such a hope, we are very bold, not like Moses, who would put a veil over his face so that the Israelites might not gaze at the outcome of what was being brought to an end. But their minds were hardened. For to this day, when they read the old covenant, that same veil remains unlifted, because only through Christ is it taken away. Yes, to this day whenever Moses is read a veil lies over their hearts. But when one turns to the Lord, the veil is removed. Now the Lord is the Spirit, and where the Spirit of the Lord is, there is freedom. And we all, with unveiled face, beholding the glory of the Lord, are being transformed into the same image from one degree of glory to another. For this comes from the Lord who is the Spirit.*

Notice the familiar themes of freedom and the Spirit.

Paul quotes Genesis 21:10 to exhort the Galatians to rid their church of these false teachers. They will not inherit with the free children and need to be driven out.

> 31 *So, brothers, we are not children of the slave but of the free woman.*

One of the main burdens of chapters three and four is to answer the questions: who are Abraham's children? Who has the rights of inheritance? Who are the people of God? He concludes his argument from allegory with this clear assertion: we are the children of the free woman. This is the same thing he said in Galatians 3:7: "Know then that it is those of faith who are the sons of Abraham;" and Galatians 3:29: "And if you are Christ's, then you are Abraham's offspring, heirs according to promise;" and Galatians 4:28:

"Now you, brothers, like Isaac, are children of promise;" and what he will say in Galatians 6:15-16: "For neither circumcision counts for anything, nor uncircumcision, but a new creation. And as for all who walk by this rule, peace and mercy be upon them, and upon the Israel of God."

Consider the contrasts used in this allegory of the two covenants:

- slave woman/free woman
- Ishmael/Isaac
- according to flesh/through promise
- Hagar/Sarah
- slavery/freedom
- present Jerusalem/Jerusalem above
- persecuting/persecuted

5:1 *For freedom Christ has set us free; stand firm therefore, and do not submit again to a yoke of slavery.*

Here we have a concluding statement and transitional statement to the next section. Christ set us free with the goal of freedom. John 8:36 says, "So if the Son sets you free, you will be free indeed." "Yoke" was often used to refer to the law. For example, in Acts 15:10, Peter says, "Now, therefore, why are you putting God to the test by placing a yoke on the neck of the disciples that neither our fathers nor we have been able to bear?"

Do you recall how Jesus used the notion of yoke? In Matthew 11:28-30, Jesus said, "Come to me, all who labor and are heavy laden, and I will give you rest. Take my yoke upon you, and learn from me, for I am gentle and lowly in heart, and you will find rest for your souls. For my yoke is easy, and my burden is light."

Notice that this verse says, "do not submit *again* to a yoke of slavery." But, one might object, the Gentiles were never under the yoke of the law. Remember though, that for Paul, "from the perspective of being 'in Christ,' Judaism and paganism could be lumped together under the rubric 'the basic principles of the world'."[133]

In this verse, we also observe the gospel logic yet again. In essence, Paul says, "You are free. Therefore be free." Christ has set us free, so stay free. One finds this gospel logic all over the New Testament. I made the same point in noting that the first imperative of the letter does not come until chapter four verse twelve. In Romans, Paul lays out eleven chapters of gospel theology before he says, *"I appeal to you therefore,"* and then goes on to lay out the practical implications of the theology. Christianity must always be distinguished from moralism. The differences are vast.

Application

- The law does not lead to freedom. We have seen this again and again. The law cannot liberate. It was never meant to. The old covenant only demanded and sinners can't keep its demands. The old covenant was just that—*old.* It was part of the old order. It lacked the power of the Spirit. One application of this truth bears on parenting. Just as in all of life, the law does not transform in parenting as well. The law increases sin. Even the secular world realizes this. Hence the saying, "Rules were meant to be broken." Now, I am not saying our children should have no

---

[133] Longenecker, *Galatians,* 225.

rules. Not at all. I believe in Genesis 3. But, we should not simply be laying down the law all the time. We must parent with the gospel.[134] Of course we need guidelines and norms, but our parenting must be grace-based.

- What should we think about Paul's allegorical interpretation? Is it a model we can follow? Yes and no. Paul's approach to allegory is unlike most allegorical approaches. In verses 21-23, Paul is simply making observations about the narrative in Genesis. He does not deny its historicity. In verse 24-27 however, he leaves the plain sense of the text to construct the allegory. Also, he tells us that they can be interpreted allegorically. If a person decides to interpret a passage allegorically, they should let the hearers know, as Paul does. Generally speaking, I think our main approach to applying the Old Testament to us or Christ is by way of typology. Typology differs from allegory in that it requires biblical warrant for making a connection. For example, there is no biblical warrant for saying that Rahab's scarlet cord is the blood of Christ, while there is biblical warrant for saying that the temple was a type of Christ. The "temple" theme really begins in Eden, and is developed through the Tent of Meeting to the Tabernacle to the Temple to the Second Temple to Christ himself then to church. Christ comes and "tabernacles" among us (John 1:14). He says of his body, "Destroy

---

134 See William P. Farley, *Gospel-Powered Parenting* (Philipsburg, NJ: P&R Publishing, 2009).

this temple, and in three days I will raise it up" (John 2:19). So we have biblical warrant for claiming that the temple was a type of Christ.[135] Without such warrant, the Old Testament can become a wax nose.

- Read the Old Testament in light of the New Testament's interpretation.[136] In this section, Paul quotes from Isaiah 54, which is in the middle of the promises of a new exodus and new creation. These realities have dawned in the resurrection of the Messiah.
- Stand firm in the freedom Christ brings. Never add to the gospel. The natural tendency of our hearts is to add to what God requires. Legalism is a universal problem, for as we saw, Satan is its main evangelist.

---

[135] For a detailed and technical study on typology, see Richard M. Davidson, *Typology in Scripture* (Berrien Springs, MI: Andrews University Press, 1981).

[136] Again, the Anabaptists had it right. See William Estep, *The Anabaptist Story* (Grand Rapids: Eerdmans, 1996), 22, 97, 126.

Chapter 10: Galatians 5:2-15

Passage

Look: I, Paul, say to you that if you accept circumcision, Christ will be of no advantage to you. I testify again to every man who accepts circumcision that he is obligated to keep the whole law. You are severed from Christ, you who would be justified by the law; you have fallen away from grace. For through the Spirit, by faith, we ourselves eagerly wait for the hope of righteousness. For in Christ Jesus neither circumcision nor uncircumcision counts for anything, but only faith working through love. You were running well. Who hindered you from obeying the truth? This persuasion is not from him who calls you. A little leaven leavens the whole lump. I have confidence in the Lord that you will take no other view than mine, and the one who is troubling you will bear the penalty, whoever he is. But if I, brothers, still preach circumcision, why am I still being persecuted? In that case the offense of the cross has been removed. I wish those who unsettle you would emasculate themselves! For you were called to freedom, brothers. Only do not use your freedom as an opportunity for the flesh, but through love serve one another. For the whole law is fulfilled in one word: "You shall love your neighbor as yourself." But if you bite and devour one another, watch out that you are not consumed by one another.

We continue the practical application section of the letter, but it is important to keep in mind that the whole letter is doctrinal. Although this is considered the practical application section of the letter, chapters five and six are a vital part of the argument of the letter as a whole.

2 *Look: I, Paul, say to you that if you accept circumcision, Christ will be of no advantage to you.*

After a couple of chapters of theology, the main issue is finally brought up: circumcision. Again, Paul wants his hearers to understand their issues theologically. He builds a theological foundation before addressing the main concern. He is not a moralist, but a Christian.

Paul has an "all or nothing" mindset concerning this issue. If you accept circumcision, you take the whole law with it. If you put yourself back under the law, Christ will be of no advantage for you. The sacrifices of the old covenant are no longer effective, so to turn back now will result in condemnation. This is why Paul is afraid that he may have labored over them in vain (Gal 4:11). We see the same idea throughout the book of Hebrews.

> 3 *I testify again to every man who accepts circumcision that he is obligated to keep the whole law.*

He testifies as in court; it is a very solemn warning. "If you don't follow me, you will be damned." When Paul says "again," he is probably referring back to Galatians 3:10: For all who rely on works of the law are under a curse; for it is written, "Cursed be everyone who does not abide by all things written in the Book of the Law, and do them."[137] Both verses use the infinitive *"poiēsai,"* which means "to do." In Galatians 5:3, the ESV translates *poiēsai* as "to keep." Now that the old covenant sacrifices are no longer available outside of Christ, one must be perfect to gain eschatological salvation. One must do the whole law (Gal 5:3).[138] One must abide by all things written in the law

---

[137] Schreiner, *Galatians*, 283.

[138] As Wright says, "Torah does not permit picking and choosing," *Justification*, 137.

and do them (Gal 3:10). Of course, this poses a major problem because no one is able to do so. The Judaizers themselves can't keep it, as Paul says in 6:13: "For even those who are circumcised do not themselves keep the law."

Again we see from this verse that the law is a unity. In Galatians 4:21, Paul said, "you who desire to be under the law." As mentioned before, for the Bible, there is no dividing up the law. To be circumcised is to be under the law. If one is circumcised, they are now obligated to do it all. We also see this perspective from Acts 15:5, which says, "But some believers who belonged to the party of the Pharisees rose up and said, 'It is necessary to circumcise them and to order them to keep the law of Moses'." The verse says the Pharisees were requiring them to be circumcised and to keep the law. Luther writes,

> Some people today would bind us to certain of Moses' laws that they like best, as the false apostles wanted to do at that time. But this is not to be allowed at all. If we give Moses leave to rule over us in anything, we are bound to obey him in everything; therefore, we must not be burdened with any law of Moses. We grant that he is to be read by us and to be listened to as a prophet and a witness of Christ, and moreover, that out of him we may take examples of good laws and holy life; but we will not let him have dominion over our conscience in any way. In this respect, let him be dead and buried, and let no one know where his grave is.[139]

4 *You are severed from Christ, you who would be justified by the law; you have fallen away from grace.*

---

[139] Luther, *Galatians,* 247.

They have fallen from grace because they are now left on their own. The sacrificial system has been done away with in the coming of Jesus, the final sacrifice. To seek justification through the law is to fall away from grace. God was gracious in the old covenant through the sacrificial system, but now that the new covenant has been ratified, the old covenant is obsolete, to use the language of another New Testament writer (Heb 8:13).

Romans 7:6 says, "But now we are released from the law, having died to that which held us captive, so that we serve in the new way of the Spirit and not in the old way of the written code." Those who have died to the law have been released *(katargēō)* from it. In Galatians 5:4, we see that to seek justification by the law results in being severed or "released" *(katargēō)* from Christ.[140]

> 5 *For through the Spirit, by faith, we ourselves eagerly wait for the hope of righteousness.*

It is only by the Spirit that we have faith. It is only by the Spirit that we look away from ourselves to trust in another. Left to our own flesh, we would always look to our own performance. We wait for the hope of righteousness by faith. Paul says we "eagerly await" (*apekdekōmai*). This verb is used often with reference to Christian hope:

> Romans 8:19 *For the creation waits* (apekdekōmai) *with eager longing for the revealing of the sons of God.*

140 S.M. Baugh, "Galatians 5:1-6 and Personal Obligation: Reflections on Paul and the Law," in *The Law is Not of Faith* (Phillipsburg, NJ: P&R Publishing, 2009), 276-77.

Romans 8:23 *And not only the creation, but we ourselves, who have the firstfruits of the Spirit, groan inwardly as we wait eagerly* (apekdekōmai) *for adoption as sons, the redemption of our bodies.*

Romans 8:25 *But if we hope for what we do not see, we wait* (apekdekōmai) *for it with patience.*

1 Corinthians 1:7 *so that you are not lacking in any spiritual gift, as you wait* (apekdekōmai) *for the revealing of our Lord Jesus Christ,*

Philippians 3:20 *But our citizenship is in heaven, and from it we await* (apekdekōmai) *a Savior, the Lord Jesus Christ,*

Hebrews 9:28 *so Christ, having been offered once to bear the sins of many, will appear a second time, not to deal with sin but to save those who are eagerly waiting* (apekdekōmai) *for him.*

Does this verse teach future justification? It depends on what one means by future justification. It clearly says we are *waiting* for the hope of righteousness (*dikaiosynē*). This is a reference to the last day, public declaration of what is now ours. We have already been justified by faith (Rom 5:1), but justification is fundamentally an end-time declaration. The beauty of the gospel is that this end-time declaration has been pronounced in the present *through faith*. God has made the declaration in advance. There is therefore *now* no condemnation for those in Christ Jesus (Rom 8:1). Westminster Shorter Catechism question 38 puts it nicely:

> Q. 38. What benefits do believers receive from Christ at the resurrection?
>
> A. At the resurrection, believers being raised up in glory, shall be openly acknowledged and acquitted in the day of

judgment, and made perfectly blessed in the full enjoying of God to all eternity.[141]

6 For in Christ Jesus neither circumcision nor uncircumcision counts for anything, but only faith working through love.

The Galatians may have misunderstood Paul and concluded that there is virtue in *not* being circumcised, but Paul wants to be clear: neither circumcision nor uncircumcision counts for anything.[142] This is one of the fundamental "rules" of the gospel. In 1 Corinthians 7:19, Paul says, "For neither circumcision counts for anything nor uncircumcision, but keeping the commandments of God." We see this same "rule" in Galatians 6:15: "For neither circumcision counts for anything, nor uncircumcision, but a new creation."[143] Notice the parallel with Galatians 5:6 and 6:15. Neither circumcision nor uncircumcision means anything, but faith working through love and the new creation counts for everything!

It is faith working through love that counts for everything! Saving faith *always* goes public in acts of obedi-

---

[141] *The Westminster Confession of Faith* (Atlanta: Committee for Christian Education & Publications, 1990), 14. Alternatively, "the hope of righteousness" may refer to the hope which our righteousness secured. See Fee, *God's Empowering Presence,* 419. Wright says, "The Christian looks *back* and celebrates the verdict already issued over faith: 'righteous,' 'my child.' The Christian looks *forward* and waits, in faith and hope, for that verdict to be announced once more on the last day," *Justification,* 139.

[142] Fee, *God's Empowering Presence,* 420.

[143] Fee, *God's Empowering Presence,* 419.

ence.[144] It always expresses itself.[145] Love is the result of faith. This is why love is considered a fruit of the Spirit (Gal 5:22). Faith is the root and love is the fruit. Elsewhere, Paul can speak of the "work of faith" (1 Thess 1:3). Work comes from faith. Interestingly, Paul sandwiches the book of Romans with the phrase "the obedience of faith" (Rom 1:5, 16:26). This is what the Apostle is calling the nations to: the obedience which flows from faith. Speaking of faith, Luther writes, "It is not idle but occupied and exercised, working through love. Paul therefore, in this verse, sets forth the whole life of a Christian—namely, that inwardly it consists in faith toward God, and outwardly in loving works to our neighbor."[146]

> 7-10 *You were running well. Who hindered you from obeying the truth? This persuasion is not from him who calls you. A little leaven leavens the whole lump. I have confidence in the Lord that you will take no other view than mine, and the one who is troubling you will bear the penalty, whoever he is.*

Paul uses racing imagery here, but also makes an allusion to circumcision. Here the NIV is better than the ESV:

---

[144] See Thomas R. Schreiner, *Run to Win the Prize* (England: Apollos, 2009); Scott J. Hafemann, *The God of Promise and the Life of Faith* (Wheaton, IL: Crossway, 2001).

[145] As the Anabaptist Balthasar Hubmaier wrote, "Such faith cannot remain passive but must break out to God in thanksgiving and to mankind in all kinds of works of brotherly love," Henry C. Wedder, *Balthasar Hubmaier* (New York: G.P. Putnam's Sons, 1905), 69-70 quoted in William R. Estep, *The Anabaptist Story* (Grand Rapids: Eerdmans, 1996), 197

[146] Luther, *Galatians,* 254

"Who cut in on you and kept you from obeying the truth?" The Galatians were being hindered from obeying the truth. No doubt, the word *truth* here refers back to Galatians 2:14, where Paul said that Peter was not keeping in step with the "truth" of the gospel. John Barclay writes, "Clearly the 'truth' that Paul expounds in the course of Galatians 2-4 is not to be given merely intellectual assent: it is meant to be 'obeyed' and to determine the pattern of their 'walk'."[147] In verse 9, he uses a proverbial statement to say that small matters have a tendency to become large matters, and can dominate. He uses the same statement in 1 Corinthians 5:6 in the context of church discipline. First Corinthians 5:7 says, "Cleanse out the old leaven that you may be a new lump." Recall that in Galatians 4:30, Paul exhorted the congregation to "Cast out the slave woman and her son." False teaching will come, and it must not be tolerated.

Paul is confident that they will heed his warnings. This is similar to the perspective of the author of Hebrews. After warning them, he has this to say: "Though we speak in this way, yet in your case, beloved, we feel sure of better things—things that belong to salvation" (Heb 6:9). This is the way warnings function in the New Testament. We all must heed them and God will use them effectively in the lives of his people. The elect always heed the warnings.[148]

Here, Paul speaks in the singular: "the one who is troubling you," but in Galatians 1:7 he spoke in the plural: "there are some who trouble you." Here, Paul may be re-

---

[147] Barclay, *Obeying the Truth*, 94.

[148] See Schreiner, *Run to Win the Prize*.

ferring to one of the leaders of the Judaizers or he may just be making a general use of the singular.

> 11 *But if I, brothers, still preach circumcision, why am I still being persecuted? In that case the offense of the cross has been removed.*

The opponents were probably accusing Paul of hypocrisy. They were probably saying that Paul continued to preach circumcision, but Paul asks, "If I still preach circumcision, why I am I still being persecuted?" If he still preached circumcision, the cross would no longer be offensive. Tom Schreiner writes, "Circumcision nullifies the scandal of the cross because it establishes righteousness based on human ability. If righteousness comes by the law, then the goodness of human beings is celebrated and promoted. The cross, however, rejects any and all human attempts to be right with God. Righteousness is found only in what Christ Jesus has done for sinners. The message of the cross is a scandal or a stumbling block because it is an affront to human pride. Human beings take umbrage in being told that even their best works are stained with evil, that everything we do is insufficient to be right with God, and that the only basis for right-standing with God is the cross of Jesus Christ."[149]

> 12 *I wish those who unsettle you would emasculate themselves!*

Richard Longenecker says of this verse: "it is the crudest and rudest of all Paul's extant statements." The Judaizers were seeking to force the Galatians to cut off the foreskin of the penis to gain favor with God, and Paul wishes they

---

[149] Schreiner, *Galatians,* 296.

would go the whole way and cut it all off. This mutilation is pointless now that Christ has come. As noted above,

> This perspective is also clear from Philippians 3:2. The Judaizers were very concerned about being ceremonially clean, doing good, and being circumcised and Paul provocatively calls them dogs (unclean), evil doers (opposite of good), and those who mutilate the flesh *(tēn katatōmēn)*. He is saying that those who cut themselves thinking this will gain salvation are "like the frenzied prophets of Baal who were frustrated that their god would not answer their pleas" (see 1 Kin 18:28, Lev 19:28, 21:5 LXX).[150]

Surely Paul had Deuteronomy 23:1 in the back of his mind when he wrote Galatians 5:12. It says, "No one whose testicles are crushed or whose male organ is cut off shall enter the assembly of the LORD." Paul wishes they would emasculate themselves and in so doing they would be shut out from the assembly of the Lord, that is, the church. They are not welcome within the people of God.

> 13 *For you were called to freedom, brothers. Only do not use your freedom as an opportunity for the flesh, but through love serve one another.*

You are free from the old covenant, but that doesn't mean you just live however you want. As Gordon Fee puts it, "To be 'Law-less' does not mean to be lawless."[151] True freedom is *obedience*. True freedom is not without boundaries. Remember, true faith expresses itself through love (Gal 5:6). Freedom is characterized by love, service to oth-

---

[150] Thielman, *Theology of the New Testament*, 318.

[151] Fee, *God's Empowering Presence*, 437.

ers, and the Spirit.[152] As John Barclay writes, "Thus faith and freedom are by no means morally bankrupt."[153]

Also, as we will see more in the next section, we still struggle with the old age, that is, the flesh.[154] The flesh represents the weakness of human nature living on the resources of this age. William Barclay says, "The flesh is what man has made himself in contrast with man as God made him. The flesh is man as he has allowed himself to become in contrast with man as God meant him to be. The flesh stands for the total effect upon man of his own sin and of the sin of his fathers and of the sin of all men who have gone before him. The flesh is human nature as it has become through sin... The flesh stands for human nature weakened, vitiated, tainted by sin. The flesh is man as he is apart from Jesus Christ and his Spirit."[155]

Paul picks up on the Exodus story yet again. The Israelites were *freed* in order to become *servants* of the Lord:[156]

> Exodus 4:23 *and I say to you, "Let my son go that he may serve me." If you refuse to let him go, behold, I will kill your firstborn son.'"*

---

[152] Longenecker, *Galatians,* 236. Gorman writes, "To be a slave is to be mastered by love," *Cruciformity,* 222.

[153] Barclay, *Obeying the Truth,* 109.

[154] John Barclay suggests that Paul uses flesh instead of sin because the former does not have the legal connotations that the Galatians might associate with the law, *Obeying the Truth,* 111.

[155] W. Barclay, *Flesh and Spirit: An Examination of Galatians 5:19-23* (London: SCM, 1962), 22 quoted in Longenecker *Galatians,* 240.

[156] Schreiner, *Galatians,* 302.

Exodus 19:4-6 *You yourselves have seen what I did to the Egyptians, and how I bore you on eagles' wings and brought you to myself. Now therefore, if you will indeed obey my voice and keep my covenant, you shall be my treasured possession among all peoples, for all the earth is mine; and you shall be to me a kingdom of priests and a holy nation.*

Exodus 20:2 *I am the LORD your God, who brought you out of the land of Egypt, out of the house of slavery.*

Leviticus 25:42 *For they are my servants, whom I brought out of the land of Egypt; they shall not be sold as slaves.*

The Galatians, just as the Israelites, were freed by the Lord in order to become servants.

The ESV translates the second half of verse 13 as "through love serve one another." A better translation is, "through love, perform the duties of a slave towards one another."[157] Most modern translations avoid the word *slave* to avoid offense, even though that is what the word means. *Servant* softens the meaning in my opinion. Servants serve others while slaves belong to others.[158] Gordon Fee writes, "Freedom from the enslavement of Torah paradoxically means to take on a new form of 'slavery'—that of loving servant-hood to one another."[159]

These duties of a slave are to be done through love. Love is very important in this letter:

---

[157] Fee, *God's Empowering Presence*, 425.

[158] See Murray J. Harris, *Slave of Christ* (Downers Grove, IL: IVP, 1999).

[159] Fee, *God's Empowering Presence*, 426; also see Barclay, *Obeying the Truth*, 109; Gorman, *Cruciformity*, 161.

Galatians 5:6 *For in Christ Jesus neither circumcision nor uncircumcision counts for anything, but only faith working through love.*

Galatians 5:13 *For you were called to freedom, brothers. Only do not use your freedom as an opportunity for the flesh, but through love serve one another.*

Galatians 5:22 *But the fruit of the Spirit is love, joy, peace, patience, kindness, goodness, faithfulness,*

Galatians 6:10 *So then, as we have opportunity, let us do good [i.e., love] to everyone, and especially to those who are of the household of faith.*

Galatians 5:13-6:10 is really an unpacking of two main exhortations: Become slaves of one another through love (Gal 5:13) and live by the Spirit (Gal 5:16).

14-15 *For the whole law is fulfilled in one word: "You shall love your neighbor as yourself." But if you bite and devour one another, watch out that you are not consumed by one another.*

How can Paul now speak about the need to fulfill the law after all the negative statements concerning the law in Galatians chapters 3 and 4? It is important to remember that the focus of the negative statements is "narrowly confined to one issue: the role of the law in justification for the reception of the Abrahamic inheritance."[160] The New Testament cites Leviticus 19:18 as a summarizing command. Loving your neighbor fulfills the law.

In Galatians 5:14, Paul uses a different phrase than he does in Galatians 5:3, although you wouldn't know it from reading the ESV. It translates two different words as "whole" in both verses. In verse 3, Paul uses *holos* (whole).

---

160 Silva, *Galatians*, 810.

In verse 14, he uses *pas* (all). Now, translating both as "whole" is legitimate, but one misses the nuance in doing so. Paul knew what he was doing here. These passages are only 11 verses apart. The NIV is better here. They used *whole* in 5:3 and *entire* in verse 14. F.F. Bruce writes, "Whereas [*holos ho nomos*] in v 3 is the sum-total of the precepts of the law, [*ho pas nomos*] here [v 14] is the law as a whole—the spirit and intention of the law."[161]

Galatians 5:3 speaks of doing (*poiēō*) the whole (*holos*) law,[162] while 5:14 speaks of fulfilling (*plēroō*) all (*pas*) of the law. This is a very important distinction for Paul.[163] Christians are never said to "do" the law, while those under the law are obligated to "do" it:

> Rom 10:5 *For Moses writes about the righteousness that is based on the law, that the person who does* [poiēō] *the commandments shall live by them.*
>
> Gal 3:10 *For all who rely on works of the law are under a curse; for it is written, "Cursed be everyone who does not abide by all things written in the Book of the Law, and do* [poiēō] *them."*

---

161 F.F. Bruce, *Epistle to the Galatians* (Grand Rapids, MI: Eerdmans, 1981), 241.

162 The ESV uses "keep" here, which again is a legitimate translation, but Paul is a very nuanced theologian and we miss the contrast by not sticking with a consistent translation of the words he uses. A similar phenomenon happens in the NIV's various translations of flesh (*sarx).*

163 Barclay, *Obeying the Truth,* 139. Later he writes, "by using the ambiguous terminology of 'fulfillment': in this way he aligns himself with the 'purpose' of the law without implying a commitment to 'observe' all its commands," *Obeying the Truth,* 233.

Gal 3:12 *But the law is not of faith, rather "The one who does* [poiēō] *them shall live by them."*

Gal 5:3 *I testify again to every man who accepts circumcision that he is obligated to keep* [poiēō] *the whole law.*

On the other hand, where Christian behavior is discussed in relation to the law, Paul inevitably uses the word *fulfill.*[164]

Rom 8:4 *in order that the righteous requirement of the law might be fulfilled* [plēroō] *in us, who walk not according to the flesh but according to the Spirit.*

Rom 13:8 *Owe no one anything, except to love each other, for the one who loves another has fulfilled* [plēroō] *the law.*

Rom 13:10 *Love does no wrong to a neighbor; therefore love is the fulfilling* [plērōma] *of the law.*

Gal 5:14 *For the whole law is fulfilled* [plēroō] *in one word: "You shall love your neighbor as yourself."*[165]

This is why I am a New Covenant theologian. Let's put away the confessions and get out the Greek New Testament. Doug Moo writes, "Vital to understanding Paul's perspective on the law is to recognize a principal distinction in his writings between 'doing' and 'fulfilling' the law. Nowhere does Paul say that Christians are to 'do' the law, and nowhere does he suggest that any but Christians can

---

[164] John Barclay writes, "this verb-root could be said to be his favorite vocabulary in describing the Christian relationship to the law," Ibid., 139.

[165] Stephen Westerholm, "On Fulfilling the Whole Law" (Gal. 5:14)," *Svensk exegetisk årsbok* 51-52 (1986-87): 233-34; idem, *Perspectives New and Old,* 329, 435-39; Longenecker, *Galatians,* 242-43.

'fulfill' the law,"[166] Only Christians, who have been delivered from the present evil age (Gal 1:4) and have received the gift of the Spirit (Gal 3:1-5) can fulfill the law. Paul, like Jesus in Matthew 5:17, is referring to eschatological fulfillment.[167]

It is also important to recognize that in these "fulfillment of the law" passages Paul is not prescribing but *describing* Christian behavior. Ironically, those who live under the law can't do it while those who have died to the law fulfill the law.[168] Only those under the law are *required* to *do* the law, while the *result* of the obedience of those not under the law *fulfills* the law.[169] Tom Schreiner writes, "Doing the law is required for justification and is unattainable, while fulfilling the law is the consequence of justification and the result of the Spirit's work."[170] Gordon Fee writes, "The aim of Torah, which Torah was helpless to bring off, was to create a loving community in which God's own character and purposes are fulfilled as God's people love one another the

---

166 Douglas Moo, "The Law of Christ as the Fulfillment of the Law of Moses: A Modified Lutheran View," in *Five Views on Law and Gospel*, ed. Stanley N. Gundry (Grand Rapids: Zondervan, 1999), 359; idem, "The Law of Moses or the Law of Christ," in John S. Feinberg, ed., *Continuity and Discontinuity: Perspectives on the Relationship Between the Old and New Testaments* (Wheaton, IL: Crossway Books, 1988), 210.

167 Fee, *God's Empowering Presence*, 614.

168 Meyer, *The End of the Law*, 283.

169 Westerholm, "On Fulfilling the Whole Law," 235.

170 Schreiner, *Galatians*, 304.

way he loves them....The Spirit has 'replaced' Torah by fulfilling the aim of Torah."[171]

Richard Longenecker makes three points concerning Paul and the law:[172]

> 1. Paul never derives appropriate Christian conduct by simply applying relevant precepts from Torah
>
> 2. Paul never claims that Christians "do" (*poiein*) the law; they—and they alone—are said to "fulfill" (*plēroun*) it.
>
> 3. Paul never speaks of the law's fulfillment in prescribing Christian conduct, but only while describing its results.

Clearly, Paul knew about conflict within the Galatian churches (Gal 5:15).[173] We see that from this passage, and by the fact that eight of the fifteen sins mentioned in chapter five are sins of discord within the community.[174] The flesh manifests itself in community strife. The verb *bite* is often used in the Old Testament for serpents (Gen 49:17, Num 21:6, 8, 9, Deut 8:15, Ecc 10:8, 11, Amos 5:19, 9:3, Jer 8:17),[175] so Paul may be saying they are acting in a demonic manner by striving against one another. The conflict may be a result of the confusion caused by the false teachers. On the other hand, there may have been community conflict first, making it easier for the false teachers to come in and distort the gospel.

---

[171] Fee, *God's Empowering Presence,* 426.

[172] Longenecker, *Galatians,* 243.

[173] Barclay, *Obeying the Truth,* 168.

[174] Fee, *God's Empowering Presence,* 424.

[175] Schreiner, *Galatians,* 305.

Application

- Christianity is not moralism (5:2). We have seen this again and again in Galatians. Theology *matters.* Behavior always has a theological foundation. Doctrine is laid out before the imperatives come.
- Without Christ, you must keep the whole law (5:3). We have also seen this again and again. The sacrificial system is obsolete now. If one looks away from Christ alone for salvation they must be flawless, and *no one* is flawless.
- Christians should be characterized by eager waiting (5:5). How eager is your waiting? America is blessed in that we are free to worship in air conditioned buildings with padded seats. Most Americans are rich compared to the rest of the world. This is both a blessing and a curse. Part of the way our context hinders us is by making us too comfortable in this world. We tend to think we have all we need here. Our waiting is not eager enough because quite frankly, we like it here. How often do you pray for the Lord's return?
- Faith is never alone. Many today equate faith with intellectual assent. Saving faith includes intellectual assent but also includes much more. Ask yourself, "Is your faith working?" If not, it may not be biblical faith. Faith *always* goes public in acts of obedience.
- Expect persecution. The cross says people are sinners in need. It says we can't save ourselves. This is a message that will never become popular.

- Biblical freedom has boundaries. Don't think that because we are no longer under law that we don't have any commandments to obey. We will unpack this more at Galatians 6:2. In this section, Paul warns us not to use our freedom as an opportunity for the flesh. Freedom does not mean autonomy.
- Love, for in this all the law is fulfilled.

Chapter 11:
Galatians 5:16-26

Passage

But I say, walk by the Spirit, and you will not gratify the desires of the flesh. For the desires of the flesh are against the Spirit, and the desires of the Spirit are against the flesh, for these are opposed to each other, to keep you from doing the things you want to do. But if you are led by the Spirit, you are not under the law. Now the works of the flesh are evident: sexual immorality, impurity, sensuality, idolatry, sorcery, enmity, strife, jealousy, fits of anger, rivalries, dissensions, divisions, envy, drunkenness, orgies, and things like these. I warn you, as I warned you before, that those who do such things will not inherit the kingdom of God. But the fruit of the Spirit is love, joy, peace, patience, kindness, goodness, faithfulness, gentleness, self-control; against such things there is no law. And those who belong to Christ Jesus have crucified the flesh with its passions and desires. If we live by the Spirit, let us also walk by the Spirit. Let us not become conceited, provoking one another, envying one another.

As mentioned above, Galatians 5:13-6:10 is really an unpacking of two main exhortations: Serve one another through love (Gal 5:13) and walk by the Spirit (5:16).[176]

> 16 *But I say, walk by the Spirit, and you will not gratify the desires of the flesh.*

In verse 13 of chapter 5, Paul had warned the Galatians not to use their freedom as an opportunity for the flesh, and now he unpacks how. If they walk by the Spirit, they will certainly not (*ou mē*) gratify the desires of the flesh.

---

[176] Longenecker, *Galatians*, 247.

This is not a command not to gratify the desires of the flesh but a promise. When walking by the Spirit, you *will not* gratify the desires of the flesh.

"Walk" (*peripateō*) is Paul's favorite verb when dealing with behavior. Christians often ask other Christians, "How is your walk?" This is very appropriate and something I think Paul would ask. Consider the many ways he uses this verb when dealing with Christian conduct:

> Romans 6:4 *We were buried therefore with him by baptism into death, in order that, just as Christ was raised from the dead by the glory of the Father, we too might* ***walk*** *in newness of life.*
>
> Romans 8:4 *in order that the righteous requirement of the law might be fulfilled in us, who* ***walk*** *not according to the flesh but according to the Spirit.*
>
> Romans 13:13 *Let us* ***walk*** *properly as in the daytime, not in orgies and drunkenness, not in sexual immorality and sensuality, not in quarreling and jealousy.*
>
> Romans 14:15 *For if your brother is grieved by what you eat, you are no longer* ***walking*** *in love. By what you eat, do not destroy the one for whom Christ died.*
>
> 1 Corinthians 3:3 *for you are still of the flesh. For while there is jealousy and strife among you, are you not of the flesh and behaving* [**walking**] *only in a human way?*
>
> 1 Corinthians 7:17 *Only let each person lead* [lit. **walk**] *the life that the Lord has assigned to him, and to which God has called him. This is my rule in all the churches.*
>
> 2 Corinthians 4:2 *But we have renounced disgraceful, underhanded ways. We refuse to practice* [lit. **walk** in] *cunning or to tamper with God's word, but by the open statement of the truth we would commend ourselves to everyone's conscience in the sight of God.*
>
> 2 Corinthians 5:7 *for we* ***walk*** *by faith, not by sight.*

2 Corinthians 10:2 *I beg of you that when I am present I may not have to show boldness with such confidence as I count on showing against some who suspect us of* ***walking*** *according to the flesh.*

2 Corinthians 10:3 *For though we* ***walk*** *in the flesh, we are not waging war according to the flesh.*

2 Corinthians 12:18 *I urged Titus to go, and sent the brother with him. Did Titus take advantage of you? Did we not act [lit.* ***walk****] in the same spirit? Did we not take the same steps?*

Galatians 5:16 *But I say,* ***walk*** *by the Spirit, and you will not gratify the desires of the flesh.*

Ephesians 2:2 *in which you once* ***walked****, following the course of this world, following the prince of the power of the air, the spirit that is now at work in the sons of disobedience—*

Ephesians 2:10 *For we are his workmanship, created in Christ Jesus for good works, which God prepared beforehand, that we should* ***walk*** *in them.*

Ephesians 4:1 *I therefore, a prisoner for the Lord, urge you to* ***walk*** *in a manner worthy of the calling to which you have been called,*

Ephesians 4:17 *Now this I say and testify in the Lord, that you must no longer* ***walk*** *as the Gentiles do, in the futility of their minds.*

Ephesians 5:2 *And* ***walk*** *in love, as Christ loved us and gave himself up for us, a fragrant offering and sacrifice to God.*

Ephesians 5:8 *for at one time you were darkness, but now you are light in the Lord.* ***Walk*** *as children of light*

Ephesians 5:15 *Look carefully then how you* ***walk****, not as unwise but as wise,*

Philippians 3:17 *Brothers, join in imitating me, and keep your eyes on those who* ***walk*** *according to the example you have in us.*

Philippians 3:18 *For many, of whom I have often told you and now tell you even with tears,* ***walk*** *as enemies of the cross of Christ.*

Colossians 1:10 *so as to **walk** in a manner worthy of the Lord, fully pleasing to him, bearing fruit in every good work and increasing in the knowledge of God.*

Colossians 2:6 *Therefore, as you received Christ Jesus the Lord, so **walk** in him,*

Colossians 3:7 *In these you too once **walked**, when you were living in them.*

Colossians 4:5 ***Walk** in wisdom toward outsiders, making the best use of the time.*

1 Thessalonians 2:12 *we exhorted each one of you and encouraged you and charged you to **walk** in a manner worthy of God, who calls you into his own kingdom and glory.*

1 Thessalonians 4:1 *Finally, then, brothers, we ask and urge you in the Lord Jesus, that as you received from us how you ought to **walk** and to please God, just as you are doing, that you do so more and more.*

1 Thessalonians 4:12 *so that you may **walk** properly before outsiders and be dependent on no one.*

2 Thessalonians 3:6 *Now we command you, brothers, in the name of our Lord Jesus Christ, that you keep away from any brother who is **walking** in idleness and not in accord with the tradition that you received from us.*

2 Thessalonians 3:11 *For we hear that some among you **walk** in idleness, not busy at work, but busybodies.*

When believers walk by the Spirit, they do not gratify the desires of the flesh. Flesh, once again, represents the weakness of human nature. It represents living on the resources of this age.[177] It is who you were before and outside

[177] John Barclay takes *sarx* as that which is merely human, *Obeying the Truth*, 209.

of Christ.[178] It is who you are in Adam. Flesh and Spirit represent eschatological realities. Flesh represents the old age and Spirit represents the new. Gordon Fee writes,

> To live 'according to the flesh' is to live in keeping with the values and desires of life in the present age that stand in absolute contradiction to God and his ways. Hence the ultimate contrasts in Paul are eschatological: life 'according to the flesh,' lived according to the present age that has been condemned through the cross and is passing away, or life 'according to the Spirit,' lived in keeping with the values and norms of the coming age inaugurated by Christ through his death and resurrection and empowered by the eschatological Spirit.[179]

This walking by the Spirit was one of the promises of the new covenant. Ezekiel 36:26-27 says, "And I will give you a new heart, and a new spirit I will put within you. And I will remove the heart of stone from your flesh and give you a heart of flesh. And I will put my Spirit within you, and cause you to walk in my statutes and be careful to obey my rules."

Gordon Fee calls "walking by the Spirit" Paul's "basic ethical imperative."[180] What does it mean to walk by the Spirit? We will see from verse 18 that it is to be led by the Spirit, and from verses 22 and following that it is bearing

---

[178] Fee, *God's Empowering Presence,* 430.

[179] Ibid., 431. See Romans 8.

[180] Ibid., 422. I appreciate this emphasis, but think "love" may be even more basic. This command occurs only here. Of course to love is to walk by the Spirit and to walk by the Spirit is to love.

the fruit of the Spirit. We will see that Paul emphasizes the work of the Holy Spirit, but that our activity is required as well. There are both active and passive aspects to walking by the Spirit.

> 17 *For the desires of the flesh are against the Spirit, and the desires of the Spirit are against the flesh, for these are opposed to each other, to keep you from doing the things you want to do.*

The flesh and the Spirit are at odds. They are opposed to one another. They are in conflict with one another (NIV). Our desires are divided in this overlap of the ages. Tom Schreiner writes, "Believers are indwelt by the Holy Spirit, and hence the promised gift of the age to come is now theirs. And yet the present evil age has not passed away (1:4). The flesh remains a reality as well, and its desires are not absent."[181]

John Barclay writes, "The Galatians need have no fear that Paul's talk of 'freedom' and 'following the Spirit' will leave them without moral direction in a structureless existence 'doing whatever they want'."[182] The absence of the law does not mean one is free to do whatever one pleases. They must now do as the Spirit leads.[183]

---

[181] Schreiner, *Galatians,* 312.

[182] Barclay, *Obeying the Truth,* 115.

[183] Richard Longenecker writes, "the flesh and 'the Sprit' are diametrically opposed to one another, with the result that one cannot do what he or she knows to be right when in 'the flesh' (*i.e.,* when living only humanly according to one's own guidance and the direction of whatever is simply human) but only when in 'the Spirit' (*i.e.,* when living in the new reality of being 'in Christ' and directed by God's Spirit)," *Galatians,* 245.

We see a similar struggle in Romans 7:14-25.[184] There Paul writes, "For I do not understand my own actions. For I do not do what I want, but I do the very thing I hate (15)…For I do not do the good I want, but the evil I do not want is what I keep on doing" (19).

18 *But if you are led by the Spirit, you are not under the law.*

Verses 16-17 tie up 5:13 and verse 18 ties up 5:14. In Galatians 5:13, Paul brought up the flesh, warning about using the freedom Christ brings as an opportunity for the flesh. In Galatians 5:16, he explains that walking by the Spirit is the key. In Galatians 5:14, Paul said that love fulfills the law. Now, in Galatians 5:18, he says that we are not under the law if we are led by the Spirit.

Walk by the Spirit and you will not gratify the flesh. Be led by the Spirit and you are not under law. This side of the resurrection, both the flesh and the law are on the same side. They are both part of the old age. Gordon Fee writes, "Thus for Paul both flesh and Torah belong to the old aeon, whose essential power has been crippled by Christ's death and resurrection, which marked the dawning of the new aeon, the time of the Spirit."[185] The Spirit is the response to

---

[184] Luther, *Galatians,* 269; Longenecker says that Gal 5:17 sets out Rom 7:14-25 in rudimentary fashion, *Galatians,* 246.

[185] Fee, *God's Empowering Presence,* 422. Later he writes, "believers who walk by the Spirit do so because they are following where the Spirit leads; and the Spirit leads in 'the law of Christ,' in ways that both reflect and pattern after Christ himself—whom Paul has earlier described as 'the one who loved me and gave himself for me' (2:20)….The framework for all of this is Paul's eschatology, in which he sees Christ and Spirit

both the flesh and the Law because the Law could not counteract the flesh, but the Spirit can and does.[186]

Paul, like in so many other places, is employing a salvation-historical argument here.[187] He does the same thing in Romans 6:14: "For sin will have no dominion over you, since you are not under law but under grace."

> 19-21 *Now the works of the flesh are evident: sexual immorality, impurity, sensuality, idolatry, sorcery, enmity, strife, jealousy, fits of anger, rivalries, dissensions, divisions, envy, drunkenness, orgies, and things like these. I warn you, as I warned you before, that those who do such things will not inherit the kingdom of God.*

The works of the flesh are evident; they are plain to all; they are obvious. How do I know if I am walking by the Spirit or by the flesh? Paul lays out representative lists to help us know. In light of Galatians 5:15[188] and 5:26,[189] it is

---

as setting the future in motion in such a way that neither circumcision nor uncircumcision has relevance, since 'the new creation' has come (6:15; cf. 2 Cor 5:17). For him the Spirit is the principal evidence of this new eschatological existence that 'eagerly awaits' its consummation (Gal 5:5). This means that everything before Christ, which was fundamentally eliminated by his death and resurrection and the gift of the eschatological Spirit, belongs to the same 'old age' sphere of existence. In that sense the Spirit stands over against both the flesh and the Law, in that he replaces the latter and stands in opposition to the former," 438.

[186] Ibid., 428; See also 438.

[187] Schreiner, *Galatians*, 314-15.

[188] "But if you bite and devour one another, watch out that you are not consumed by one another."

not surprising that eight of the fifteen sins listed are related to community strife.[190] Contrary to popular understanding, this section is not simply about you and your relationship with the Lord. Rather, "the concern from beginning to end is with Christian life in community, not with the interior life of the individual Christian."[191] Christianity is fundamentally *communal.*

Paul begins the list with sexual immorality, probably due to the fact that the Greco-Roman world's view of sex was characterized by lawless chaos, much like present-day America.[192] Idolatry is the root sin for the apostle Paul. Romans 1 tells us that the fundamental problem with humanity is a failure to thank and praise God and to turn to the creation rather than the creator (Rom 1:21-25).[193] Paul mentions that he had taught them these things before. He is reminding them of the seriousness of these sins. Those who "practice" (*prassō)* (NAS) or "live like this" (NIV) will not inherit the kingdom of God. Obviously, we are not talking about simply doing one of these sins once. No, Paul is worried about what characterizes a person's life. We all stumble in many ways (James 3:2), but there is a difference between falling into sin, and diving into it.

---

189 "Let us not become conceited, provoking one another, envying one another."

190 Fee, *God's Empowering Presence,* 423.

191 Ibid., 425.

192 Longenecker, *Galatians,* 254.

193 Schreiner, *Galatians,* 316.

When Paul says they will not "inherit" the kingdom, we cannot forget what he has already said about "heirs":

Gal 3:29 *And if you are Christ's, then you are Abraham's offspring, heirs according to promise.*

Gal 4:7 *So you are no longer a slave, but a son, and if a son, then an heir through God.*

Gal 4:30 *But what does the Scripture say? "Cast out the slave woman and her son, for the son of the slave woman shall not inherit with the son of the free woman."*

Paul is not simply saying, "Avoid these vices and you will inherit the kingdom." He has already said one becomes an heir by being united to The Heir (Gal 3:16) through faith. But we must always remember that faith for Paul is never static. It is dynamic. It works through love (Gal 5:6).

22-23 *But the fruit of the Spirit is love, joy, peace, patience, kindness, goodness, faithfulness, gentleness, self-control; against such things there is no law.*

Paul uses the metaphor of fruit to describe the virtues of the new life in Christ. Again, this is not an exhaustive list. Paul could have added such virtues as generosity, hospitality, perseverance, thankfulness, and humility to name a few. I have always found the metaphor of fruit interesting. He could have said the vegetable of the Spirit, but I don't think it would have had the same effect. Most people enjoy fruit. It is sweet and refreshing.

David Dockery writes, "Paul may well have derived the metaphor of fruitfulness or unfruitfulness from the OT. There Israel is compared to a fruit-bearing tree or vineyard (e.g., Ps 80:8-18; Is 5:1-7; 27:2-6; Jer 2:21; 11:16; 12:10; Hos 14:6; cf. 4 Ezra 9:31-32), and Isaiah can bring indictment against the 'vineyard' of the Lord for not bearing its righteous fruit (Is 5:2, 4). When Israel is restored, however, and the Spirit is poured out, the land will be fruitful (Is 32:15-16), and the trees and vine will bear their fruit (Joel 2:18-32)."[194] Consider the language of two such passages:

> Isaiah 32:15 *until the Spirit is poured upon us from on high, and the wilderness becomes a fruitful field, and the fruitful field is deemed a forest. Then justice will dwell in the wilderness, and righteousness abide in the fruitful field.*

> Joel 2:22-32 *Fear not, you beasts of the field, for the pastures of the wilderness are green; the tree bears its fruit; the fig tree and vine give their full yield. "Be glad, O children of Zion, and rejoice in the LORD your God, for he has given the early rain for your vindication; he has poured down for you abundant rain, the early and the latter rain, as before. "The threshing floors shall be full of grain; the vats shall overflow with wine and oil. I will restore to you the years that the swarming locust has eaten, the hopper, the destroyer, and the cutter, my great army, which I sent among you. "You shall eat in plenty and be satisfied, and praise the name of the LORD your God, who has dealt wondrously with you. And my people shall never again be put to shame. You shall know that I am in the midst of Israel, and that I am the LORD your God and there is none else. And my people shall never again be put to shame. "And it shall come to pass afterward, that I will pour out my Spirit on all flesh; your sons and your daughters shall prophesy, your old men shall dream dreams, and your young men shall see visions. Even on the male and female servants in those days I will pour out my Spirit. "And I will show wonders in the heavens and on the earth, blood and fire and columns of smoke. The sun shall be turned to darkness, and the moon to blood, before the great and awesome day of the*

---

[194] D.S. Dockery, "Fruit of the Spirit," in *Dictionary of Paul and His Letters* (Downers Grove, IL: IVP, 1993), 317.

LORD comes. And it shall come to pass that everyone who calls on the name of the LORD shall be saved.[195]

The church, the children of Abraham (Gal 3:7, 29), the restored Israel (6:16) has received the end-time gift of the Spirit (Acts 2) and is bearing fruit.

This is a list of virtues, which shows that Paul is more concerned with the *character* of the actor than on the duties of the actor. As John Barclay writes, "his concern is with the display of moral character, not simply the observance of a set of duties. In this connection it may be significant that Paul uses the singular 'fruit', and describes the Christian's activity as his 'work' (singular, 6:4). His concern is for the fundamental direction of a person's life, which may be demonstrated in a plethora of activities but cannot be simply equated with them."[196] Barclay is insightful here. The Holy Spirit's concern is with the fundamental direction of a person's life. Just as committing one of the sins in the vice list one time does not damn a person, so bearing one of the virtues listed doesn't guarantee inheritance. No, Paul is showing the *type* of character kingdom people have (cf. Matt 5-7).

Love is the first fruit listed. Love is *central* to the Christian life. It is the direct result of first being loved by God, who is love. It is the heart and soul of the Christian ethic (1 Thess 3:12, 4:9-10, 1 Cor 13:1-13, 16:14, Rom 13:8-10, Col 3:14, Eph 5:2).[197] But love must be defined biblically. As

---

[195] Barclay, *Obeying the Truth,* 121; Schreiner, *Galatians,* 318.

[196] Ibid., 231.

[197] Schreiner, *Galatians,* 319.

N.T. Wright says, "The English word 'love' is trying to do so many different jobs at the same time that someone really ought to sit down with it and teach it how to delegate."[198] I love my wife and I love Chinese food. Obviously there is a difference between these two types of love. Love is not simply an emotion, but self-giving action for the benefit of others.[199] Tom Schreiner defines love as "giving oneself for others, so that they are encouraged and strengthened to give themselves more fully to God."[200] Love is helping a person glorify God. This being the case, Paul's rebuke of the false teachers is loving. It is what they most need, even though they do not realize it.

Love is a central focus of the letter:[201] The only thing that matters is faith working through *love* (Gal 5:6). We are called to perform the duties of a slave towards one another through *love* (Gal 5:13). The whole law is fulfilled in one word: You shall *love* your neighbor as yourself (Gal 5:14). Colossians 3:12-14 says, "Put on then, as God's chosen ones, holy and beloved, compassionate hearts, kindness, humility, meekness, and patience, bearing with one another and, if one has a complaint against another, forgiving each other; as the Lord has forgiven you, so you also must

---

198 N.T. Wright, *After You Believe: Why Christian Character Matters* (New York: HarperOne, 2010), 183

199 Dockery, "Fruit of the Spirit," 318. Fee says it is "self-sacrificially giving oneself for others," *God's Empowering Presence,* 447. Gorman says "love is characterized by self-giving for the good of others," *Cruciformity,* 160.

200 Schreiner, *Galatians,* 319.

201 Gorman, *Cruciformity,* 219.

forgive. And above all these put on love, which binds everything together in perfect harmony." Tom Schreiner is probably right to suggest that Colossians 3:14 may mean that love is the bond that holds all the virtues together.[202]

Love stands at the head because it is the exact opposite of most of the vices listed in verses 19-21. As Paul wrote elsewhere, "Love is patient and kind; love does not envy or boast; it is not arrogant or rude. It does not insist on its own way; it is not irritable or resentful; it does not rejoice at wrongdoing, but rejoices with the truth. Love bears all things, believes all things, hopes all things, endures all things" (1 Cor 13:4-7).

Joy is the true mark of knowing God. Christians are to rejoice always (1 Thess 5:16, Phil 4:4). The community of Christ is to be characterized by peace, well-being, and wholeness. We are all sinners and therefore need patience (or forbearance) with one another. Even when sinned against, the people of God must be kind. This isn't simply referring to having nice thoughts, but to showing *acts* of kindness to one another. Goodness is closely aligned with kindness, which are both expressions of love. In Galatians 6:10, Paul tells us to do good to everyone, especially our brothers and sisters. We are to bear the fruit of faithfulness, both to God and to one another, just as to love God is to love our neighbor. Gentleness, according to Gordon Fee, carries the sense of humility (a proper self-perception) and considerateness toward others.[203] And finally, believers must exercise self-control.

---

[202] Ibid.

[203] Fee, *God's Empowering Presence*, 452.

The phrase "against such things there is no law" (*kata tōn toioutōn ouk estin nomos*) may mean that the law is unable to produce such virtues due to hardness of heart and the lack of the Spirit (cf. 2 Cor 3).[204] Or it may mean, in line with Galatians 5:14, that such things fully satisfy the law's requirements.[205] But it probably simply means that there is no law against such virtues. The law does not exist against virtues but against vices. When walking in the Spirit, you *will* love your neighbor. You won't need anyone to tell you not to murder, etc.[206]

> 24 *And those who belong to Christ Jesus have crucified the flesh with its passions and desires.*

Believers have crucified the flesh. This is similar to what Paul wrote in Galatians 2:20: "I have been crucified with Christ." The *I* here is who we were in Adam. It is the old self. He is dead. This is also similar to what Paul wrote in Romans 6:4: "Likewise, my brothers, you also have died to the law through the body of Christ." By being united to Christ in baptism, we have died to the law. We have also died to the flesh because of our union with the crucified Christ. Again we see that both the flesh and the law are part of the old age.

But how can we still struggle with the flesh if we have crucified the flesh? The answer is found, *once again*, in the gospel and its implications. It is found in the indicative and the imperative. Similarly, in Romans 6:2, Paul says we have

---

[204] Schreiner, *Galatians*, 320.

[205] Longenecker, *Galatians*, 263.

[206] Fee, *God's Empowering Presence*, 453.

died to sin, but in Romans 6:11 he commands us to consider ourselves dead to sin. The commands flow from the gospel realities. Christ has set us free, so be free (Gal 5:1)! You are dead to sin, reckon it so (Rom 6:11)! You have crucified the flesh (Gal 5:24) so walk by the Spirit and you will not gratify the desires of the flesh (Gal 5:16)!

John Piper has a very helpful analogy of a mortally wounded dragon to describe the flesh:

> "Picture your flesh—that old ego with the mentality of merit and craving for power and reputation and self-reliance—picture it as a dragon living in some cave of your soul. Then you hear the gospel, and in it Jesus Christ comes to you and says, "I will make you mine and take possession of the cave and slay the dragon. Will you yield to my possession? It will mean a whole new way of thinking and feeling and acting." You say: "But that dragon is me. *I* will die." He says, "And you will rise to newness of life, for I will take its place; I will make my mind and my will and my heart your own." You say, "What must I do?" He answers, "Trust me and do as I say. As long as you trust me, we cannot lose." Overcome by the beauty and power of Christ you bow and swear eternal loyalty and trust. And as you rise, he puts a great sword in your hand and says, "Follow me." He leads you to the mouth of the cave and says, "Go in, slay the dragon." But you look at him bewildered, "I cannot. Not without you." He smiles. "Well said. You learn quickly. Never forget: my commands for you to do something are never commands to do it alone." Then you enter the cave together. A horrible battle follows and you feel Christ's hand on yours. At last the dragon lies limp. You ask, "Is it dead?" His answer is this: "I have come to give you new life. This you received when you yielded to my possession and swore faith and loyalty

> to me. And now with my sword and my hand you have felled the dragon of the flesh. It is a mortal wound. It will die. That is certain. But it has not yet bled to death, and it may yet revive with violent convulsions and do much harm. So you must treat it as dead and seal the cave as a tomb. The Lord of darkness may cause earthquakes in your soul to shake the stones loose, but you build them up again. And have this confidence: with my sword and my hand on yours this dragon's doom is sure, he is finished, and your new life is secure."
>
> I think that is the meaning of verse 24, "Those who belong to Christ have crucified the flesh with its passions and desires." Christ has taken possession of our soul. Our old self has been dealt a mortal wound and stripped of its power to have dominion. The Christian life, the fruit of the Spirit, is a constant reckoning of the flesh as dead (piling stones on its tomb) and a constant relying on the present Spirit of Christ to produce love, joy, and peace within. The difference between the Christian life and popular American morality is that Christians will not take one step unless the hand of Christ holds the hand that wields the sword of righteousness."[207]

The flesh and its desire are still present, but they no longer have dominion.

25-26 *If we live by the Spirit, let us also walk by the Spirit. Let us not become conceited, provoking one another, envying one another.*

In Galatians 3:3, Paul asked the Galatians "Are you so foolish? Having begun by the Spirit, are you now being

---

[207] John Piper, "Walk by the Spirit!", accessed from http://www.desiringgod.org/ResourceLibrary/Sermons/ByScripture/7/399_Walk_by_the_Spirit/ on 8/10/2010.

perfected by the flesh?" He concludes this section by saying in essence, "You have begun by the Spirit, now continue to keep in step with the Spirit (not the flesh)." The first word should be translated *if,* not *since* (contra NIV). Paul wants to put a bit of pressure on his readers, so they will examine themselves. Here again we have gospel logic. Paul could have used the same verb in both clauses: If we live by the Spirit, let us live by the Spirit. Paul's ethic could be summarized as, "Become in your character and conduct what God has made you to be in Christ."

So we see there are passive and active elements to our Christian walk. We are commanded to walk by the Spirit (5:16), be led by the Spirit (5:18), and keep in step with the Spirit (5:25). When we do these things, there will be no conceit, provocation, or envy in the community.

Application

- Walk—not run—by the Spirit. As we saw, this is Paul's favorite verb to use when discussing ethical behavior. He could have said "Run by the Spirit" but progress is often slow in this overlap of the ages.
- Life is war. The desires of the flesh remain. You never remain in the same place. One is either growing closer to the Lord, or falling away from the Lord. There is no room for standing still in the Christian life. Character is formed over the long haul. Christ-conformity occurs over hundreds and hundreds of small steps in the right direction. *Walk* by the Spirit.

- Be patient with growth. I love the title of one of Eugene Peterson's books: *A Long Obedience in the Same Direction.*[208] The always pastoral Luther writes,

> Do not be surprised, then, when you feel this battle of the sinful nature against the Spirit. Pluck up you courage, and comfort yourself with these words of Paul, which tell you that it is impossible to follow the guiding of the Spirit without any hindrance by the sinful nature. The sinful nature will resist you so that you cannot do what you would gladly do. It will be enough, then, if you follow the Spirit and not your sinful nature, which is easily overthrown by impatience, seeks revenge, holds grudges, hates God, is angry with him, despairs , and so on. Therefore, when you feel this battle, do not be discouraged, but resist in the Spirit and say, 'I am a sinner, and I feel sin in me, for I have not yet put off the sinful nature. But I will obey the Spirit and not my sinful nature. I will by faith and hope lay hold upon Christ, and by his Word I will raise myself up and will not do what my sinful nature desires.[209]

- A Christian is not a person who never wrestles with sinful desires. A Christian is a person who is at war with those desires by the power of the Spirit. Inner conflict is not all bad. Indeed, it shows the fact that the Spirit of God dwells in you. In the midst of the battle, don't gaze at your own navel but look outside of yourself to the risen Christ and to your neighbors in loving service.
- There is a war to wage, but we are new covenant believers. There should be significant and observable

---

[208] Downers Grove, IL: IVP, 1980.

[209] Luther, *Galatians,* 271.

progress in holiness. We should see victory over sin in our lives. We have the Spirit, the very presence of God dwelling within us!

- Fruit grows gradually. You can't see fruit grow immediately but you can over time. Often you don't feel it. Often, you can't tell you have grown until some trial occurs. Fruit is seasonal. Growth is often slow, but inevitable. If you have the Spirit, you *will* have change.
- These are communal sins and virtues. Swim against our post-Enlightenment, American, self-centered individualism. Be other-centered, just as our Savior was (Phil 2).

Chapter 12: Galatians 6:1-10

Passage

Brothers, if anyone is caught in any transgression, you who are spiritual should restore him in a spirit of gentleness. Keep watch on yourself, lest you too be tempted. Bear one another's burdens, and so fulfill the law of Christ. For if anyone thinks he is something, when he is nothing, he deceives himself. But let each one test his own work, and then his reason to boast will be in himself alone and not in his neighbor. For each will have to bear his own load. One who is taught the word must share all good things with the one who teaches. Do not be deceived: God is not mocked, for whatever one sows, that will he also reap. For the one who sows to his own flesh will from the flesh reap corruption, but the one who sows to the Spirit will from the Spirit reap eternal life. And let us not grow weary of doing good, for in due season we will reap, if we do not give up. So then, as we have opportunity, let us do good to everyone, and especially to those who are of the household of faith.

The Apostle is still unpacking Galatians 5:13 (perform the duties of a slave for one another through love) and 5:16 (walk by the Spirit and you will not gratify the desires of the flesh). He now explains the fruit of the Spirit in everyday life.

> 1 *Brothers, if anyone is caught in any transgression, you who are spiritual should restore him in a spirit of gentleness. Keep watch on yourself, lest you too be tempted.*

We still battle with the flesh, and we will be caught in transgression at times. When another gets caught in a sin, we are called to restore them gently. When Paul says, "you who are spiritual," he is not referring to an elite group, but to all of them. You who, in line with Galatians 5:25, live by the Spirit should restore sinners in a spirit of gentleness.[210]

Notice that here he commands a virtue that he had previously said was a fruit of the Spirit (Gal 5:23).[211] There are both active and passive elements to the Christian life. As we are led by the Spirit, we bear the fruit of the Spirit while at the same time Paul *commands* us to be gentle. Paul was no doubt familiar with Jesus' teaching in Matthew 18:15-16: "If your brother sins against you, go and tell him his fault, between you and him alone. If he listens to you, you have gained your brother. But if he does not listen, take one or two others along with you, that every charge may be established by the evidence of two or three witnesses."

When you restore a brother or sister, remember your own susceptibility to temptation. Always keep your own frailty in mind. As we have seen again and again, there is no room for self-righteousness in the Christian life. We are reminded of Jesus' teaching, this time in Matthew 7:3-5: "Why do you see the speck that is in your brother's eye, but do not notice the log that is in your own eye? Or how can you say to your brother, 'Let me take the speck out of your eye,' when there is the log in your own eye? You hypocrite,

---

[210] Fee, *God's Empowering Presence,* 461. There he writes, "With this word he is not, as some would have it, addressing a special group within the community who are, or think they are, 'spiritual,' who must restore a fallen one because he or she is (presumably) not 'spiritual.' In such a case, Paul would surely have said '*those* who are spiritual.' Rather, Paul is addressing the whole community ('*you* who are spiritual)."

[211] Ibid., 462.

first take the log out of your own eye, and then you will see clearly to take the speck out of your brother's eye."

2-5 *Bear one another's burdens, and so fulfill the law of Christ. For if anyone thinks he is something, when he is nothing, he deceives himself. But let each one test his own work, and then his reason to boast will be in himself alone and not in his neighbor. For each will have to bear his own load.*

With the words *law* and *fulfill,* Galatians 6:2 points back to 5:14, but it should be noted that Paul uses different verbs in these verses.[212]

What is the law of Christ? In short, it is the ethical standard of the new covenant. It is worth taking a moment to clarify what Paul has in mind here. As we step back for a minute, consider what has been made clear thus far. Paul has clearly shown us that new covenant believers are not under law. One cannot read chapters three and four without seeing that leaping off the pages. We have also seen that Paul expects his hearers to behave in a certain way. Just because believers are not under law, does not mean they are to use their freedom as an opportunity for the flesh. Paul has exhorted the Galatians to walk by the Spirit. Now he introduces the law of Christ. Doubtless, the Galatians would have known what Paul was referring to. He had instructed them previously so that now he simply mentions it in passing.

Paul uses a similar phrase in 1 Corinthians 9:20-21. There he wrote:

---

[212] 5:14 *plēroō;* 6:2 *ana plēroō*. See Fee, *God's Empowering Presence,* 463-64.

> *To the Jews I became as a Jew, in order to win Jews. To those under the law I became as one under the law (though not being myself under the law) that I might win those under the law. To those outside the law I became as one outside the law (not being outside the law of God but under the law of Christ) that I might win those outside the law.*

This passage is so helpful for clarifying the relationship of new covenant believers to the law. We are not under the law, a fact that should be very obvious by now. Yet, we are not outside the law of God. This is so important. For Paul (and therefore for us) the Mosaic law is not equivalent to the law of God in the new covenant era! So what is the law of God for the new covenant age? The law of Christ. Read those verses again. We are not under the law, but aren't outside God's law; we are in-lawed to Christ (*ennomos Christou*).

Elsewhere, I have defended a five point definition.[213] The law of Christ is:

1. The law of love

We already noted the parallel between Galatians 6:2 and Galatians 5:13-14. Just from these two passages we can see that the law of Christ is love of neighbor. The whole law is fulfilled in loving your neighbor and the law of Christ is fulfilled in bearing one another's burdens.[214] We get the same perspective from Paul's writings in Romans 13:8-10, which says,

---

[213] A. Blake White, *The Law of Christ: A Theological Proposal* (Frederick, MD: New Covenant Media, 2010).

[214] Keller, *Galatians,* 176

Owe no one anything, except to love each other, for the one who loves another has fulfilled the law. For the commandments, "You shall not commit adultery, You shall not murder, You shall not steal, You shall not covet," and any other commandment, are summed up in this word: "You shall love your neighbor as yourself." Love does no wrong to a neighbor; therefore love is the fulfilling of the law.

In Matthew 22, a Pharisee asks Jesus which commandment in the law is the great one. Jesus replies,

And he said to him, "You shall love the Lord your God with all your heart and with all your soul and with all your mind. This is the great and first commandment. And a second is like it: You shall love your neighbor as yourself. On these two commandments depend all the Law and the Prophets." (Matt 22:37-40)

So Augustine had meditated on this passage when he made the famous statement that anyone who claims to know any part of the Holy Scriptures so that it fails to produce this double love of God and neighbor, actually knows nothing of the Scriptures. James 2:8 similarly says, "If you really fulfill the royal law according to the Scripture, 'You shall love your neighbor as yourself,' you are doing well." Do well brothers and sisters, and love your neighbor, and so fulfill the law of Christ.

2. The example of Jesus

Jesus is the one who shows us what love is, especially in the cross.[215] Previously in Galatians, Paul had written that this Christ *gave himself* for our sins (Gal 1:4). Jesus loved us

---

215 So Gorman defines the law of Christ as "the narrative pattern of self-giving, others-regarding love of the crucified Messiah Jesus," *Cruciformity*, 174.

and gave himself for us (Gal 2:20). Love finds its truest expression in *this* Jesus, the self-giving Messiah, who lays down his life for the good of others. The cross provides an example for believers. We are to walk in love, as Christ has loved us and gave himself up for us (Eph 5:2). Jesus is our Savior, absolutely, but he is *also* our example! He submitted to the Father and accepted suffering for the good of others. We are to imitate him (2 Cor 8:9, 1 Cor 11:1, 1 Thess 1:6, Phil 1:27-2:13).

This aspect of the cross tends to get neglected in "conservative" circles. The less conservative tends to attack the substitutionary nature of the cross so conservatives have spent most of their effort refuting such attacks (rightly so). The imbalance comes when other aspects of the cross are neglected and the breadth of the cross is missed. Christ was punished in our place for our sins *and* provides an example for our lives in doing so.

Consider Philippians 2:3-11:

> *Do nothing from rivalry or conceit, but in humility count others more significant than yourselves. Let each of you look not only to his own interests, but also to the interests of others. Have this mind among yourselves, which is yours in Christ Jesus, who, though he was in the form of God, did not count equality with God a thing to be grasped, but made himself nothing, taking the form of a servant, being born in the likeness of men. And being found in human form, he humbled himself by becoming obedient to the point of death, even death on a cross. Therefore God has highly exalted him and bestowed on him the name that is above every name, so that at the name of Jesus every knee should bow, in heaven and on earth and under the earth, and every tongue confess that Jesus Christ is Lord, to the glory of God the Father.*

Here we have some glorious doctrine: Christology, incarnation, deity, and kenosis, but don't get distracted. Paul's point in mounting up all the Christology is *so that* his hearers will count others better than themselves. He could have stopped there, but he grounds his exhortation in the self-giving of the Messiah. We are to have this mind among us. In Romans 15:1-3, Paul is exhorting the strong to bear with the failings of the weak. He wants the strong to worry about pleasing the weak rather than pleasing themselves. Then he grounds his exhortation this way: "For *[gar]* Christ did not please himself."

John 13:34-35 is one of my life verses and is important for this point. It says, "A new commandment I give to you, that you love one another: just as I have loved you, you also are to love one another. By this all people will know that you are my disciples, if you have love for one another." The commandment is new because we have the example of Christ.

3. The teaching of Jesus

I hold this truth to be self-evident.[216] Christians are to adhere to the teachings of Jesus. In Deuteronomy 18:15-18,

---

[216] Although self- evident, the teaching of Jesus is often neglected in Reformation circles. The Gospels are often read through Pauline lenses instead of vice-versa. This area is where the Reformed tradition(!) can learn from the Anabaptist tradition. Stuart Murray writes, "The Protestant reformers honored Jesus as the one through whose redeeming work sinful human beings could be justified, but they generally paid scant attention to his life and teaching. They read Paul's letters avidly but were not particularly interested in the Gospels… The re-

Moses speaks of a coming prophet like him, to whom the people will listen. Using similar language, Luke 9:35 records the Father saying of Jesus, "This is my Son, my Chosen One; listen to him!" In the famous "Great Commission" of Matthew 28, we read:

> *And Jesus came and said to them, "All authority in heaven and on earth has been given to me. Go therefore and make disciples of all nations, baptizing them in the name of the Father and of the Son and of the Holy Spirit, teaching them to observe all that I have commanded you. And behold, I am with you always, to the end of the age."* (Matt 28:18-20)

---

formers agreed with Anabaptists that Jesus was 'the source of our life,' but it seems clear that it was the death of Jesus, rather than Jesus himself, who was at the center of their faith… [the Anabaptists] provoked the reformers, who thundered the centrality of Jesus for salvation but seemed reticent about allowing Jesus' life and teaching to be normative for lifestyle, church, and mission. For the Anabaptists, being Jesus-centered was a choice of ultimate loyalties, but the reformers seemed reluctant to risk the wrath of the political authorities by applying his teaching to social and economic issues… The teaching of Jesus is watered down, privatized, and explained away. Jesus is worshipped as a remote kingly figure or a romanticized personal savior. In many churches (especially those emerging from the Reformation), Paul's writings are prioritized over the Gospel accounts of the life of Jesus. And in many Christian traditions, ethical guidelines derived from the Old Testament or pagan philosophy trump Jesus' call to discipleship," in *The Naked Anabaptist* (Scottdale, PA: Herald Press, 2010), 55-56.

Part of making disciples is teaching them to observe all that Jesus commanded. The law of Christ obviously includes his own teaching.

4. The teaching of the Apostles

The relationship of Jesus to his apostles is a very tight one. Jesus commissions them (see John 14-16). Earlier in the letter to the Galatians, Paul wrote, "For I would have you know, brothers, that the gospel that was preached by me is not man's gospel. For I did not receive it from any man, nor was I taught it, but I received it through a revelation of Jesus Christ" (Gal 1:11-12). The law of Christ includes the teaching of Christ's apostles, which we have in the form of the New Testament.

5. The teaching of the whole canon interpreted in light of the coming of Christ

At the end of the day, the law of Christ includes the whole Bible *interpreted in light of Christ.*[217] As New Testament scholar Richard Hays puts it, "Within the canon the New Testament has a privileged hermeneutical function...

[217] As the Anabaptists put it at the Bern Disputation of 1538, "We believe in and consider ourselves under the authority of the Old Testament, in so far as it is a testimony of Christ; in so far as Jesus did not abolish it; and in so far as it serves the purpose of Christian living. We believe in and consider ourselves under the authority of the Law in so far as it does not contradict the new law, which is the Gospel of Jesus Christ. We believe in and consider ourselves under the authority of the prophets in so far as they proclaim Christ," Jan P. Matthijssen, "The Bern Disputation of 1538," MQR 22 (January 1948), 30 quoted in Estep, *The Anabaptist Story,* 191-92.

Christian theology reads the Old Testament through the lens of the New Testament."[218] As the Anabaptists insisted, we learn exegesis from the apostles.[219]

We see this perspective from Matthew chapter five. Jesus did not come to abolish the law, but to fulfill (*plēroō)* it. "Fulfill" is used thirteen times in Matthew in reference to the Old Testament and in context should be interpreted as "bringing to pass that to which it pointed." In this sense the law was prophetic (see Matt 11:13, Rom 3:21). The law remains normative, but must be interpreted in light of Christ, who brings to pass what the law pointed to.

In our discussion of Galatians, I hope it has been clear that we are no longer under the old covenant. It is vitally important, however, to insist that this does not mean we are no longer bound by the Old *Testament*. The old *covenant* is not the same thing as the Old *Testament*. The old covenant was given at Sinai while the Old Testament refers to the whole of the Hebrew Scriptures.[220]

The famous test case for the law's relation to new covenant believers is the Sabbath. The Sabbath is really the main reason for difference between Covenant Theology and New Covenant Theology. I believe the Sabbath is eternally binding on me, but I *define the Sabbath differently* than

---

218 Richard Hays, *The Moral Vision of the New Testament* (New York: HarperOne, 1996), 309.

219 See Estep, *The Anabaptist Story*, 22, 97, 126, 192, 194, 196; Murray, *The Naked Anabaptist*, 63, 68.

220 I realize *testament* is a translation of *covenant*, but in our day, we refer to the "Old Testament" as the 39 books in our canon preceding the "New Testament."

Covenant Theology defines it. I obey the Sabbath by believing in the Lord of the Sabbath (Matt 11:28-12:8) and entering eschatological salvation rest (Heb 3:7-4:14). There is no evidence for the Sabbath as a creation ordinance. There is no evidence for shifting the Sabbath from Saturday to Sunday. Here our Seventh Day Adventist friends are more consistent in their "covenant theology." As we saw above, the ten words cannot be extrapolated from the covenant of which they were given.[221]

It takes care, humility, discernment, and wisdom to apply the law to new covenant believers. An easy example is the command to build a parapet around one's roof (Deut 22:8). An application for us is putting a "Beware of Dog" sign on our fence or building a fence around a swimming pool to protect life. That's the heart of the command, is it not? An application of the year of Jubilee (Lev 25) could be to "have all things in common" as the early church did (Acts 2:44). An application of Exodus 21 on personal injury laws could be the prohibition of abortion. We know that an application of Deuteronomy 25:4 on not muzzling an ox when it is treading grain is to pay workers their due (1 Cor 9:9-10). The examples are numerous.

Now, let's get back to the specifics of Galatians 6. In Galatians 6:3, Paul is alluding back to 5:26, where he had exhorted the Galatians to avoid becoming conceited.[222] The boasting mentioned in verses 3-5 is not for this life, but is

---

[221] For a fantastic study on the Sabbath and all the theological implications, see *From Sabbath to Lord's Day*, ed. D.A. Carson (Eugene, OR: Wipf and Stock Publishers, 1982).

[222] Schreiner, *Galatians*, 331.

end-time boasting.[223] We see this also in 1 Thessalonians 2:19, where Paul wrote, "For what is our hope or joy or crown of boasting before our Lord Jesus at his coming? Is it not you" (cf. 1 Cor 4:5)? On the last day, you stand alone. Each one will have to bear his own load. Paul had previously used this verb *bear* (*bastazō*) in Galatians 5:10: "I have confidence in the Lord that you will take no other view than mine, and the one who is troubling you will bear the penalty, whoever he is." He is referring to final judgment.[224]

> 6 *One who is taught the word must share all good things with the one who teaches.*

Paying teachers is important in the New Testament. Consider 1 Corinthians 9:14, which says, "In the same way, the Lord commanded that those who proclaim the gospel should get their living by the gospel." First Timothy 5:17 says, "Let the elders who rule well be considered worthy of double honor, especially those who labor in preaching and teaching. For the Scripture says, "You shall not muzzle an ox when it treads out the grain," and, "The laborer deserves his wages"." (cf. Matt 10:10, Luke 10:7). The verb *share (koinōnēō)* is used in other places to refer to financial provisions:

> Romans 12:13 *Contribute* (koinōnēō) *to the needs of the saints and seek to show hospitality.*

> Philippians 4:15 *And you yourselves also know, Philippians, that at the first preaching of the gospel, after I departed from Mace-*

---

[223] Ibid., 332.

[224] Ibid., 333.

donia, no church shared (koinōnēō) *with me in the matter of giving and receiving but you alone; (NAS).*

The noun (*koinōnia*) is also used in reference to financial provision:

Rom 15:26 *For Macedonia and Achaia have been pleased to make some contribution* (koinōnia) *for the poor among the saints at Jerusalem.*

2 Cor 8:4 *begging us earnestly for the favor of taking part* (koinōnia) *in the relief of the saints—*[225]

"Good things" refers to the basic necessities of life (financial support).[226] Note how Luke uses the same word:[227]

Luke 12:18 *And he said, 'I will do this: I will tear down my barns and build larger ones, and there I will store all my grain and my goods.* [19] *And I will say to my soul, Soul, you have ample goods laid up for many years; relax, eat, drink, be merry.'*

Luke 16:25 *But Abraham said, 'Child, remember that you in your lifetime received your good things, and Lazarus in like manner bad things; but now he is comforted here, and you are in anguish.*

So pay your teachers because false teachers will come in. The church needs men devoted to the study of the Scriptures. As Tom Schreiner writes, "Those being taught are exhorted to support financially those who teach the Word, presumably so that the teachers can invest the requisite time and energy for study and proclamation."[228]

7 Do not be deceived: God is not mocked, for whatever one sows, that will he also reap.

---

[225] Ibid., 337.

[226] Keller, *Galatians*, 186.

[227] Schreiner, *Galatians*, 337.

[228] Ibid., 337.

In 2 Corinthians 9:6-7, Paul uses the same metaphor to refer to financial giving: "The point is this: whoever sows sparingly will also reap sparingly, and whoever sows bountifully will also reap bountifully. Each one must give as he has decided in his heart, not reluctantly or under compulsion, for God loves a cheerful giver." Do you mock God by how you use your money? You will reap what you sow. Do not be deceived. Paul used similar language in 1 Corinthians 6:9, which says, "Or do you not know that the unrighteous will not inherit the kingdom of God? Do not be deceived." He wants to make sure that we are not deceiving ourselves. Living unrighteously, which in this context means sowing to the flesh, results in corruption (*i.e.*, not inheriting the kingdom of God).

> 8 *For the one who sows to his own flesh will from the flesh reap corruption, but the one who sows to the Spirit will from the Spirit reap eternal life.*

If you sow to the flesh (*i.e.*, you use your worldly goods on yourself and in accord with selfish desires),[229] you will be damned. Paul says that how you *spend* your money is related to where you *spend* eternity. Did you hear that? It bears repeating for American ears: *the one who sows to his own flesh will from the flesh reap corruption.* If you sow to the Spirit, which in context is still focusing on generous giving, you will reap eternal life.[230] This is similar to what he stated

---

[229] Ibid., 338.

[230] Fee argues that to sow to the Spirit is to walk by the Spirit, be led by the Spirit, bear the fruit of the Spirit, and keeping in step with the Spirit. Surely this is true, but contextually the

in Galatians 5:19-21: if you practice the works of the flesh you will not inherit the kingdom of God. If you regularly sow to the flesh, you will *not* be saved. Is Paul teaching works-based salvation here? Scripture teaches that saints must *persevere.* Obedience is necessary for salvation, but is not the *basis* of salvation. Protestants must take good works seriously if we are going to take Scripture seriously. Saving faith *always* works through love (Gal 5:6). As Luther put it, "If such works do not follow faith, it is a sure sign that their faith is not true faith. Hence the apostle says, 'The one who sows to please his sinful nature—that is, who gives nothing to the ministers of God's Word but only feeds and cares for himself—that person will reap corruption not only in this life, but also in the life to come'."[231]

9-10 *And let us not grow weary of doing good, for in due season we will reap, if we do not give up. So then, as we have opportunity, let us do good to everyone, and especially to those who are of the household of faith.*

Here again we have a fruit of the spirit mentioned: goodness. The Spirit produces it, but Paul commands it of us. That is one of the many paradoxes of the Christian life. Goodness is not an abstract feeling, but an action. Again, in this context, the focus is on doing good *financially* (2 Thess 3:13). Tom Schreiner writes, "Perhaps we can say again that 'doing good' goes beyond helping others financially, but the latter seems to be the focus of the Pauline exhorta-

---

focus is still on giving *financially*. See Fee, *God's Empowering Presence,* 465.

[231] Luther, *Galatians,* 296.

tion."[232] Paul was always eager to remember the poor (Gal 2:10). We are called to do good to all, but especially to our family in Christ. We should prioritize our doing good first to our family (1 Tim 5:8), then to our local church, then to believers outside our local fellowship, then to the rest of the world. Galatians 6:10 forms an inclusion to this section with 5:13 (serve one another through love). Beautiful! How should we apply this section?

Application

- Serve through love (5:13); express your faith by working through love (5:6); walk by the Sprit (5:16); finish by the Spirit (cf. 3:3); be led by the Spirit (5:18); bear the fruit of the Spirit (5:22); sow to the Spirit (6:8); do good (6:9-10).
- Help your brothers and sisters in sin (6:1). This presupposes you are open and honest about your sin. You can't bear the burdens of others if you are unaware of them. One of the main ministries to the church one can do is attend. *Be* a member. Hang around after the service to converse with your brothers and sisters in Christ. Be hospitable. Have people over to your place; meet up for coffee. As you help erring sinners, watch yourself. As you help a brother or sister out, do not become self-righteous and fall into the same sin yourself. Sin is deceptive.
- Walking by the Spirit involves paying your teachers (6:6). Do not be deceived, God is not mocked. He sees your checkbook. Your teachers need to be able

[232] Schreiner, *Galatians*, 340.

to devote time and energy to the study of God's Word.

- "Generous giving is not optional according to Paul. It is a prime indication that one is walking in the Spirit (5:16), being led by the Spirit (5:18), and sowing to the Spirit (6:8)."[233] Don't deceive yourself. The Old Testament tithe was 23.3%. Studies have shown that American Christians give an average of less than 3%. The New Testament nowhere commands tithing, but 10% ought to be the training wheels of giving for new covenant believers.[234] There are simple principles to help free you up to give more. Live under your means to give beyond your means. Budget, avoid debt, don't simply buy because you can, simplify, distinguish between needs and wants.
- Do good to your local church and do good to everyone.

---

[233] Ibid., 341.

[234] I heard this phrase from Randy Alcorn.

Chapter 13: Galatians 6:11-18

Passage

See with what large letters I am writing to you with my own hand. It is those who want to make a good showing in the flesh who would force you to be circumcised, and only in order that they may not be persecuted for the cross of Christ. For even those who are circumcised do not themselves keep the law, but they desire to have you circumcised that they may boast in your flesh. But far be it from me to boast except in the cross of our Lord Jesus Christ, by which the world has been crucified to me, and I to the world. For neither circumcision counts for anything, nor uncircumcision, but a new creation. And as for all who walk by this rule, peace and mercy be upon them, and upon the Israel of God. From now on let no one cause me trouble, for I bear on my body the marks of Jesus. The grace of our Lord Jesus Christ be with your spirit, brothers. Amen.

The beginnings and endings of letters are important for understanding the content in the body.[235] As we saw, many of the major themes of the letter are presented in the first five verses: Paul's apostleship, the resurrection which inaugurates the new age, the fact that Paul is not alone, the cross of Christ, deliverance from the present evil age and the glory that belongs to God alone.[236] So also here at the end as well, some of the main themes are summarized.

---

[235] Longenecker, *Galatians,* 286-89.

[236] Wright remarks, "As usual, Paul opens with a summary greeting which contains a strong hint of what is to come. 'Grace to you and peace from God our Father and the Lord Jesus [the Messiah], who gave himself for our sins to set us free from the

Boast in the Cross

11-12 *See with what large letters I am writing to you with my own hand. It is those who want to make a good showing in the flesh who would force you to be circumcised, and only in order that they may not be persecuted for the cross of Christ.*

Paul says that he writes with large letters. This may be because of Paul's poor eyesight. Remember in Galatians 4:15, he reminded the Galatians that they would have gouged out their eyes and given them to him. This is simply speculation. It may simply mean that he wants to emphasize that he was serious.

The Judaizers want to make a good showing in the flesh. Their motives are not pure. We saw this previously when Paul said that they want to shut the Galatians out so they would make much of the agitators (Gal 4:17). They would force the believers there to be circumcised. Earlier in the letter, he pointed out that Titus was not *forced* to be circumcised (Gal 2:3). Peter, acting hypocritically, was *forcing* the

---

present evil age, according to the will of our God and Father, to whom be the glory forever and ever. Amen.' There we have it all: the single-plan-of-God; the eschatological framework (Jesus has broken through from the present age of sin and death into the new age, taking with him those whom he is rescuing from the latter and for the former); by implication the forensic context ('for our sins': something to do with his 'giving of himself' has, as in 1 Corinthians 15:3, had the effect of dealing with sin); and of course the central Christology, the achievement of Jesus as Messiah. And all to the praise and glory of God. All that follows will simply unpack this typically dense opening flourish," *Justification* (Downers Grove, IVP Academic, 2009), 113.

Gentiles to live like Jews (Gal 2:14). These cowards just want to avoid persecution because of the cross. Paul was being *persecuted* because of the cross of Christ (Gal 5:11). The cross says no to human ability, a fact most people take offense to.

> 13 *For even those who are circumcised do not themselves keep the law, but they desire to have you circumcised that they may boast in your flesh.*

Their view of people was too optimistic and their view of themselves was too optimistic. Even Peter should have known that Jews are just like Gentiles: persons (*anthrōpos*) in need of grace (Gal 2:15-16). All who rely on the works of the law are under a curse because no one can perfectly keep the law (Gal 3:10). Romans 3:19-20 similarly says, "Now we know that whatever the law says it speaks to those who are under the law, so that every mouth may be stopped, and the whole world may be held accountable to God. For by works of the law no human being will be justified in his sight, since through the law comes knowledge of sin." The very ones seeking to impose the law are lawbreakers themselves.

> 14 *But far be it from me to boast except in the cross of our Lord Jesus Christ, by which the world has been crucified to me, and I to the world.*

What a strange statement. The shock effect is lost on modern Christian ears. We forget the repugnance with which the cross was viewed among both Jews and Gentiles in the 1st century.[237] Death on a cross was the penalty for slaves. It symbolized shame, pain, and humiliation. It was a

---

[237] Longenecker, *Galatians,* 294.

nasty instrument of execution. This is Paul's only boast? Really, Paul? This would be akin to a modern person saying, "But far be it from me to boast in anything except lethal injection needles." You would call that person crazy. Elsewhere Paul wrote that he resolved to know nothing except Jesus Christ, that is (explicative *kai*) Jesus Christ crucified (1 Cor 2:2).

Paul uses the phrase *mē genoita* here as he has already done previously (Gal 2:17, 3:21). These two words are translated as "certainly not," "by no means," "God forbid," and "may it never be." God forbid that we boast in anything besides the cross.

This is what makes the Christ hymn of Philippians 2 all the more amazing.[238] Jesus was in the form of God but made himself nothing, taking the form of a slave by becoming obedient to death *on a cross*! This is all that Paul boasts in. By the cross, the world has been crucified to us and us to the world.

Through the crucifixion of Jesus, the world is dead to us and we are dead to the world. The world here is the old world.[239] Through the cross and resurrection, Christ has started up the new world. The green grass is peeking through the cracked concrete.

---

[238] Martin Hengel, *Crucifixion* (Philadelphia: Fortress Press, 1977), 62.

[239] Longenecker views the world as the mode of life which is characterized by earthly advantages, viewed as obstacles to righteousness, *Galatians* 295.

In chapter one, we mentioned the centrality of the cross in this short letter, and it is worth noting again:

> 1:4 *Christ gave himself for our sins*
>
> 2:20 *The Son of God loved me and gave himself for me*
>
> 3:1 *It was before your eyes that Jesus Christ was publicly portrayed as crucified*
>
> 3:13 *Christ redeemed us from the curse of the law by becoming a curse for us*
>
> 4:4-5 *God sent forth his Son to redeem those under the law*
>
> 5:1 *Christ has set us free*
>
> 5:11 *If I still preach circumcision, the offense of the cross has been removed*
>
> 6:12 *They are troubling you in order that they may not be persecuted for the cross of Christ*
>
> 6:14 *Far be it from me to boast except in the cross of our Lord Jesus Christ*

Galatians 6:14 forms an *inclusio* with Galatians 1:4 since both highlight the work of Christ on the cross. Those who belong to Christ Jesus have *crucified* the flesh (Gal 5:24). The cross delivers us from the present evil age (Gal 1:4) and the cross crucifies the old world (Gal 6:14).

> 15 *For neither circumcision counts for anything, nor uncircumcision, but a new creation.*

Verse 15 grounds verse 14. We should boast only in the cross because (*gar*) neither circumcision nor uncircumcision counts for anything, but new creation counts for everything.[240] In this verse, we find the reason for Paul's writing.

We have another *inclusio* here with Galatians 1:4. Christ delivered us from the old age (creation) and inaugurated the new creation (age). The cross, as the pivot-point of the ages, and the new creation are bound together. Circumcision, as part of the old covenant, is part of the old age. Schreiner writes, "Eschatology, then, plays a vital role in Galatians, for the Judaizers were attached to the old age and failed to see that the new had come."[241]

We have seen the phrase "neither circumcision nor uncircumcision counts for anything" previously in Galatians and as well as in 1 Corinthians:

> *For in Christ Jesus neither circumcision nor uncircumcision counts for anything, but only faith working through love.* (Gal 5:6)
>
> *For neither circumcision counts for anything nor uncircumcision, but keeping the commandments of God.* (1 Cor 7:19)

The old distinctions no longer hold up. What matters is faith working through love, keeping the commandments of God, and the new creation!

> 16 *And as for all who walk by this rule, peace and mercy be upon them, and upon the Israel of God.*

This "rule" (*kanōn*) here is the rule of the new creation: neither circumcision nor uncircumcision matters—only the new creation matters. The verb for *walk* (*stoicheō*) here is the

---

240 The TNIV translates this verse as "Neither circumcision nor uncircumcision means anything; what counts is the new creation."

241 Schreiner, *Galatians*, 350.

same one used in Galatians 5:25 for "keeping in step" with the Spirit. To keep in step with the Spirit is to keep in step with the "rule" of the new creation.[242] This is not surprising since, as we have seen, the Spirit is the gift of the new age. Isaiah 32:12-18 says:

> *Beat your breasts for the pleasant fields, for the fruitful vine, for the soil of my people growing up in thorns and briers, yes, for all the joyous houses in the exultant city. For the palace is forsaken, the populous city deserted; the hill and the watchtower will become dens forever, a joy of wild donkeys, a pasture of flocks; until the Spirit is poured upon us from on high, and the wilderness becomes a fruitful field, and the fruitful field is deemed a forest. Then justice will dwell in the wilderness, and righteousness abide in the fruitful field. And the effect of righteousness will be peace, and the result of righteousness, quietness and trust forever. My people will abide in a peaceful habitation, in secure dwellings, and in quiet resting places.*[243]

When the Spirit is poured out from on high, the wilderness will become a fruitful field. The old creation will become new. It will be a place of justice, righteousness, and peace. Israel will abide in a peaceful habitation on the new earth.[244]

Peace and mercy be upon those who follow *this* (*houtos*) rule. The phrase, *"and* (kai) *upon the Israel of God"* has proved to be controversial, but it shouldn't be. Is Paul referring to two different groups here? So it would read, "Peace be upon the new creation people (*i.e.*, the church) and peace also be upon ethnic Israel." Not a chance. This

---

[242] Ibid.

[243] Ibid., 350-51.

[244] Cf. the vision of the New Jerusalem in Revelation 21-22.

would turn the argument of the entire letter on its head. He has labored over the last six chapters to show that there *is no distinction between Jew and Gentile in Christ.* To bring a distinction into the letter at its close would utterly confuse his readers. The TNIV is better on this verse, translating the *kai* as explicative: "Peace and mercy to all who follow this rule—to the Israel of God."

Clearly he is referring to the church here, which consists of Jews and Gentiles who trust Christ.[245] We have seen this perspective in Paul's other letters:

> Romans 2:28-29 *For no one is a Jew who is merely one outwardly, nor is circumcision outward and physical. But a Jew is one inwardly, and circumcision is a matter of the heart, by the Spirit, not by the letter. His praise is not from man but from God.*
>
> Philippians 3:3 *For we are the circumcision, who worship by the Spirit of God and glory in Christ Jesus and put no confidence in the flesh—*

We have also seen it again and again in this letter:

> 3:7 *Know then that it is those of faith who are the sons of Abraham.*
>
> 3:29 *And if you are Christ's, then you are Abraham's offspring, heirs according to promise.*
>
> 4:28 *Now you, brothers, like Isaac, are children of promise.*
>
> 4:31 *So, brothers, we are not children of the slave but of the free woman.*
>
> 6:16 *And as for all who walk by this rule, peace and mercy be upon them, and upon the Israel of God.*

---

[245] Barclay, *Obeying the Truth,* 98; Longenecker, *Galatians,* 297-99; Schreiner, *Galatians,* 352-53, 362; O. Palmer Robertson, *The Israel of God* (Phillipsburg, NJ: P&R Publishing, 2000), 40-46.

As Luther put it, "In effect Paul is saying, 'The Israel of God are those who, along with faithful Abraham, believe the promises of God offered in Christ, whether they are Jew or Gentiles, and not only those who are physically descended from Abraham, Isaac, and Jacob'."[246] Long before Luther, Justin Martyr (100-165) wrote, "We have been led to God through this crucified Christ, and we are the true spiritual Israel, and the descendants of Judah, Jacob, Isaac, and Abraham."[247]

It is important to note though, that this vision of Gentiles being included in Israel is not new to the New Testament. Paul isn't making this up. For instance, Isaiah 19:16-25 says,

> *In that day the Egyptians will be like women, and tremble with fear before the hand that the LORD of hosts shakes over them. And the land of Judah will become a terror to the Egyptians. Everyone to whom it is mentioned will fear because of the purpose that the LORD of hosts has purposed against them. In that day there will be five cities in the land of Egypt that speak the language of Canaan and swear allegiance to the LORD of hosts. One of these will be called the City of Destruction. In that day there will be an altar to the LORD in the midst of the land of Egypt, and a pillar to the LORD at its border. It will be a sign and a witness to the LORD of hosts in the land of Egypt. When they cry to the LORD because of oppressors, he will send them a savior and defender, and deliver them. And the LORD will make himself known to the Egyptians, and the Egyptians will know the LORD in that day and worship with sacrifice and offering, and they will make vows to the LORD*

---

[246] Luther, *Galatians*, 303.

[247] Justin Martyr, *Dialogue with Trypho*, trans. Thomas B. Falls, ed. Michael Slusser (Washington D.C.: The Catholic University of America Press, 2003), 21.

and perform them. And the LORD will strike Egypt, striking and healing, and they will return to the LORD, and he will listen to their pleas for mercy and heal them. In that day there will be a highway from Egypt to Assyria, and Assyria will come into Egypt, and Egypt into Assyria, and the Egyptians will worship with the Assyrians. In that day Israel will be the third with Egypt and Assyria, a blessing in the midst of the earth, whom the LORD of hosts has blessed, saying, "Blessed be Egypt my people, and Assyria the work of my hands, and Israel my inheritance."

As Christopher Wright remarks, "The shock of reading 'Egypt' immediately after 'my people' (instead of the expected Israel) and of putting Israel third on the list is palpable. Yet there it is. The archenemies of Israel will be absorbed into the identity, titles and privileges of Israel and share in the Abrahamic blessing of the living God, YHWH."[248] Paul saw this reality coming into existence after the resurrection of the Messiah.

This perspective is found throughout the Old Testament. Psalm 22:27-28 says, "All the ends of the earth shall remember and turn to the LORD, and all the families of the nations shall worship before you. For kingship belongs to the LORD, and he rules over the nations." Psalm 67:1-3 says, "May God be gracious to us and bless us and make his face to shine upon us, Selah that your way may be known on earth, your saving power among all nations. Let the peoples praise you, O God; let all the peoples praise you!"

---

248 Christopher Wright, *The Mission of God* (Downers Grove, IL: IVP, 2006), 493.

In Amos 9:11-12, we read: "In that day I will raise up the booth of David that is fallen and repair its breaches, and raise up its ruins and rebuild it as in the days of old, that they may possess the remnant of Edom and all the nations who are called by my name," declares the LORD who does this.

All the nations will be called by the Lord's name! In Deuteronomy 28:9-10, we read that it is Israel that is called by the Lord's name: "The LORD will establish you as a people holy to himself, as he has sworn to you, if you keep the commandments of the LORD your God and walk in his ways. And all the peoples of the earth shall see that you are called by the name of the LORD, and they shall be afraid of you."[249] In the latter days, Gentiles will be included in the "Israel of God."

Zechariah 2:10-11 says, "Sing and rejoice, O daughter of Zion, for behold, I come and I will dwell in your midst, declares the LORD. And many nations shall join themselves to the LORD in that day, and shall be my people. And I will dwell in your midst, and you shall know that the LORD of hosts has sent me to you." Again, Wright says, "This is not 'Israel plus the nations' but 'the nations as Israel,' one people belonging to God."[250] As usual, Paul's theology here has its roots in the Hebrew Scriptures.

New Testament scholar Greg Beale argues that Galatians 6:15-16 should be understood in light of Isaiah 54:10 and the surrounding context, which is very likely seeing how

---

[249] Ibid., 496.

[250] Ibid., 498.

many times Isaiah 40 and following has been referenced by Paul throughout the letter thus far.[251] Isaiah 54:10 says, "For the mountains may depart and the hills be removed, but my steadfast love (*eleōs* LXX) shall not depart from you, and my covenant of peace (*ērēnē* LXX) shall not be removed," says the LORD, who has compassion [or mercy, so KJV] (*hileōs* LXX) on you." Galatians 6:16 says, "peace *(ērēnē)* and mercy *(eleōs)* be upon them." The context of Isaiah 54 has already been noted. Verse 10 speaks of the covenant of peace which will fulfill the previous covenants, which are alluded to all throughout chapter 54. Verses 11-12 of Isaiah 54 allude to the new creation, which is the New Jerusalem: "I will set your stones in antimony, and lay your foundations with sapphires. I will make your pinnacles of agate, your gates of carbuncles, and all your wall of precious stones."

These Isaianic promises of a new exodus, new covenant, and new creation have come to pass in the resurrection of Jesus. New creation is here. Peace and mercy be upon the eschatological Israel, who follows the rule of the new creation: neither circumcision nor uncircumcision matters.

17-18 *From now on let no one cause me trouble, for I bear on my body the marks of Jesus. The grace of our Lord Jesus Christ be with your spirit, brothers. Amen.*

Oddly enough, I have seen many people get tattoos of this verse. These marks are not referring to tattoos though, but to the marks from suffering as an apostle. Paul's apos-

---

[251] Gregory K. Beale, "Peace and Mercy Upon the Israel of God. The Old Testament Background of Galatians 6:16b." *Bib* 80 (1999): 204-23.

tolic ministry was full of suffering for the sake of Christ (Gal 5:11). He was imprisoned, beaten, often near death, with great labors, stoned, shipwrecked, constantly in danger, without sleep, without food and drink, and in daily angst for the churches all for the sake of Christ (2 Cor 11:23-30). In a sense, he tells the Galatians, "My marks are better than circumcision."[252]

Application

- Boast only in the cross. The cross is our only hope. Satan and his servants are constantly trying to divert God's people from boasting in anything besides the cross. Is the cross your only boast? Make it so.
- Understand your identity (6:16). We are the eschatological Israel. We are God's children. We are heirs according to promise.
- Know what time it is (6:15). New creation is here. We are the people of the future, called to bring God's good future into the present. The church is a sign of the new creation. The church is a foretaste of the kingdom. The church is also an instrument of God's future. We erect signposts of the new earth in the midst of this present evil age.
- What matters is the new creation (6:15). How often do you think of the new creation? It has been started up now, but we await its final consummation. Heav-

---

[252] Michael Gorman points out that in the ancient world slaves were often branded with identifying marks, known as *stigmata,* of their owner. Paul understands himself and his marks in light of this practice. See Gorman, *Cruciformity,* 147.

en will not be disembodied. Heaven is *earthy*. It is creation, just *new*. We are called to let the vision of that reality inform our thought and behavior in the present time. This is the reason Paul concludes 1 Corinthians 15 as he does. After many verses on the importance of the resurrection of Christ, which is the first fruits of our resurrection and the resurrection of the cosmos, Paul concludes with this exhortation to work in the meantime:

Therefore, my beloved brothers, be steadfast, immovable, always abounding in the work of the Lord, knowing that in the Lord your labor is not in vain.

Conclusion

Wow! I hope you have been as refreshed as I have by this magnificent letter. It is beautiful. The people of God learn so much about what it means to be the people of God from this short epistle. My prayer is that this book is an aid to that end. My aim is to help people be better readers and doers of this letter. In conclusion, Richard Longenecker's words are fitting:

> Historically Paul's letter to the Galatians has been foundational for many forms of Christian thought, proclamation, and practice. Likewise, today, how one understands the issues and teaching of Galatians determines in large measure what kind of theology one espouses, what kind of message one proclaims, and what kind of lifestyle one lives. May it be, by God's Spirit, that what Paul has written so long ago in this letter finds a new home in our lives, thereby establishing, encouraging, challenging, and transforming us for God's glory.[253]

soli deo gloria

---

[253] Longenecker, *Galatians,* 301.

www.ingramcontent.com/pod-product-compliance
Lightning Source LLC
LaVergne TN
LVHW051048080426
835508LV00019B/1759

* 9 7 8 1 9 2 8 9 6 5 3 6 7 *